GOD'S BAILOUT PLAN

(Bible-Based Financial Principles)

CAROLYN V. KEITH

Vineyard Ministry Inc, Publisher

Scripture quotations are from the King James Version of the Bible.

ACKNOWLEDGMENTS

To God be the glory. It was the Lord who directed my steps, provided wisdom and placed within my heart a burning desire to share the information contained within these pages. I pray that He is pleased and His message on finances has been clear and above all helpful. It has been a two-year journey to pull together the contents of this book. Many within my family and church played key roles in encouraging me to the finish line. Sometimes the unfinished book would be shelved for weeks at a time while other things in life took a front seat. I appreciate the love, support and encouragement that put me back on track. A special thanks to my husband, who offered invaluable insight and feedback.

Table of Contents

INTRODUCTION

Wisdom is the principle thing: therefore, get wisdom and with all thy getting, get understanding

Proverbs 4:7

During President Bush's and Obama's administrations, America faced financial turmoil. Foreclosures reached unprecedented levels, mortgages were upside down, and AIG and the auto industry were in crisis. Unemployment and the lack of affordable health insurance affected millions of households. The government provided programs, laws, and assistance to address these and many other concerns that helped immensely in ending the Great Recession. It was a terrifying and uncomfortable time for many Americans.

Bailouts for individuals and industry were developed to get America back financially. However, the financial struggle was not over. As soon as it appeared as if our financial problems had been resolved, a worldwide pandemic – COVID wreaked havoc. There were stay-at-home orders, in-person learning traded for remote learning, houses of worship closed, and over 1 million Americans lost their lives. Many lost their jobs, and several businesses closed their doors permanently. The government provided stimulus packages and other programs not only for individuals but for businesses, landlords, and churches as well. Many lenders let borrowers work out alternative payments. The government extended unemployment benefits longer than expected. However, for many, the help was too little too late.

At the time of this writing, the world is establishing its new normal. However, many businesses find that workers prefer to work remotely instead of returning to the office. Others do not want to return to work, and some workers are demanding higher wages. Many businesses need more staffing, particularly in the fast-food and retail industries. Customer service has suffered. Inflation has caused historically high gas and food prices, meaning household incomes must stretch further to meet ends.

Reflecting on all that has happened in the last twelve to sixteen years, I could not think of a more befitting title than God's Bailout Plan.

The plans or programs implemented to date to address the Great Recession and COVID did not address everyone's problems completely. Often, it made things even worse. There are many whose finances are still in turmoil due to illness, job loss, inflation, or making bad choices. Many Americans are still in need of a financial bailout. However, the bailout presented within these pages is based on Godly advice. God's guidance is timeless and works no matter what happens.

There are scriptures throughout the bible that guide us through this financial journey. Your situation can turn around even if you started on the wrong foot. Like everything else with the Lord, you are not alone. Practical advice will help you put the scriptural advice into action at each step. You didn't get where you are overnight, and your problem will likely not disappear overnight. If followed faithfully, it will provide bailout solutions for your finances.

The Lord is greatly concerned about you and all that you do. Psalm 139 describes how intimately the Lord knows you personally.

1   O Lord, thou hast searched me, & known me

2   Thou knowest my downsitting and mine uprising, thou understandest my thought afar off.

3   Thou compassest my path and my lying down, And art acquainted with all my ways.

4 For there is not a word in my tongue, But, lo, O LORD, thou knowest it altogether.

5 Thou hast beset me behind and before, And laid thine hand upon me.

6 Such knowledge is too wonderful for me; It is high, I cannot attain unto it.

7 Whither shall I go from thy spirit? Or whither shall I flee from thy presence?

8 If I ascend up into heaven, thou art there: If I make my bed in hell, behold, thou art there.

9 If I take the wings of the morning, and dwell in the uttermost parts of the sea;

10 Even there shall thy hand lead me, And thy right hand shall hold me.

11 If I say, Surely the darkness shall cover me; Even the night shall be light about me.

12 Yea, the darkness hideth not from thee; But the night shineth as the day: The darkness and the light are both alike to thee.

13 For thou hast possessed my reins: Thou hast covered me in my mother's womb.

14 I will praise thee; for I am fearfully and wonderfully made: Marvellous are thy works; And that my soul knoweth right well.

Psalm 139

According to these verses, the Lord has sent us a message of love and concern. No matter what we do or where we go, God knows all about it. No one can hide from His presence. The Lord understands your words and what you mean when you speak them. You (we) are wonderfully made by the Lord. He wants His creation to live their best lives. He does not want us to suffer. Whatever situation you find yourself in today financially, you can change it. God is the God of second, third, fourth, fifth, etc. chances.

This book can benefit 1) Those in financial turmoil. 2) Those who may have issues in one or more financial aspects and are seeking solutions, or 3) Those curious about what scripture says about finances. So whether it is a complete or partial bailout that is needed or a spiritual financial awareness, this book provides invaluable information for you.

Everyone's financial situation is riddled with customs, habits and preferences. What might be a good fit for one individual may not be for another. However, there are a number of apps and financial instruments presented as suggestions and not recommendations. They are meant to point you in the right direction. Everything mentioned is helpful to someone. Look at the apps and financial instruments and make your own assessment by selecting those items that appear to meet your individual needs. After you have made your selection, research the pros and cons associated with the item(s) selected. If the disadvantages outweigh the advantages, select something else that feels more comfortable. For example, if you would like to take advantage of savings offered via coupons but do not have time to clip them, consider Honey or some other browser extension that provides access to coupons. Let's get started. Beginning on page 15, is a Christian Financial Assessment Tool, My Spend-o-Meter. Please take up to 15 minutes to complete the assessment. When you finish reading this book and have implemented some suggestions provided, go back and revisit My Spend-o-Meter. Determine if your newfound knowledge and your change in mindset have made a difference in your scoring and your approach to finances.

> Happy is the man that findeth wisdom, and the man that getteth understanding. For the merchandise of it is better than the merchandise of silver, and the gain thereof than fine gold.
>
> Proverbs 3:13-14

MY SPEND-O-METER

EXERCISE:

YOU'VE JUST BEEN GIVEN A MONETARY GIFT OF $1,000. WHAT WILL YOU DO? WHEN YOU HAVE COMPLETED THE EXERCISE, MAKE SURE THAT YOUR TOTAL EQUALS $1,000. If you need more space, fill free to do what is needed to reach $1,000. Please complete this portion of the assessment in five minutes or less. Also if there is something you want to do with the gift and you don't know how much it costs, use your best guess.

Description	Amount
	$
	$
	$
	$
	$
	$
	$
	TOTAL: $1000

YOUR FINANCIAL DECISIONS

There are seven sections. In each section, select the statement that most closely reflects the financial decision(s) taken with the $1,000. Select only one response per section.

SECTION I : GIVING

1	I gave part of my $1,000 to my church and I do this from time to time.
2	I didn't give any of my $1,000 to any church and I never give to the church.
3	I gave 10% of my $1,000 and an offering to my church as I always do.
4	I didn't give any of the $1,000 to church this time but I give on occasion .

SECTION II : SPENDING

5	I didn't purchase anything and I didn't pay any bills. I needed some things and didn't want anything.
6	I didn't purchase anything and I didn't pay any bills. I wanted some things and didn't need anything.
7	I didn't purchase anything and I didn't pay any bills. I needed and wanted some things.
8	I didn't purchase anything and I didn't pay any bills. I didn't need or want anything.
9	I purchased what I wanted. I didn't need anything. I didn't pay bills.

10	I purchased what I wanted. I didn't purchase what I needed. I didn't pay bills.
11	I purchased what I needed. I didn't want anything. I didn't pay bills.
12	I purchased what I needed. I didn't purchase anything I wanted. I didn't pay bills.
13	I purchased some things I wanted and some things I needed. I didn't pay bills.
14	I paid bills. I didn't get anything I needed or wanted.
15	I paid bills. I purchased some things I needed and wanted.
16	I paid bills. I didn't need or want anything.
17	I paid bills. I purchased what I wanted and I didn't need anything.
18	I paid bills. I purchased what I wanted. I didn't purchase what I needed.
19	I paid bills. I purchased what I needed. I didn't want anything.
20	I paid bills. I purchased what I needed. I didn't purchase anything I wanted.
21	I don't have any bills. I purchased what I wanted. I didn't need anything.
22	I don't have any bills. I purchased what I wanted. I didn't purchase what I needed.
23	I don't have any bills. I purchased what I needed. I didn't want anything.
24	I don't have any bills. I purchased what I needed. I didn't purchase anything I wanted.
25	I don' have any bills. I purchased some things I wanted and some things I needed.
26	I don't have any bills. I didn't purchase anything. I didn't want or need anything.
27	I don't have any bills. I didn't purchase anything. I wanted some things and didn't need anything.

28	I don't have any bills. I didn't purchase anything. I needed some things and didn't want anything.
29	I don't have any bills. I didn't purchase anything. I needed and wanted some things.

SECTION III : SAVING / INVESTING

Saving or investing toward long term financial goals refer to things such as reducing credit card debt, college, retirement, vacations, new car, new house, various home projects etc. Emergency savings are funds set aside for loss of employment or other unexpected expenses.

30	I saved/ invested for emergencies and I do save from time to time.
31	I saved/invested for emergencies. I always try to save what I can, when I can.
32	I didn't save/invest anything this time for emergencies but I do save occasionally.
33	I didn't save/invest anything and I never do.
34	I saved/invested for emergencies and for my long term financial goals.
35	I saved/invested for my long term financial goals. I already had monies saved/invested for emergencies.
36	I saved/invested for my long-term financial goals. I did not save anything for an emergency.

THE NEXT FOUR SECTIONS DEAL WITH THE PROCESS YOU WOULD USE IN REAL LIFE IN PURCHASING THINGS YOU WANT OR NEED:

SECTION IV : SHOPPING - WANTS

37	When I shop for something I want, I wait until I have enough to pay for it
38	When I shop for something I want and don't have enough to purchase it, I borrow the additional funds from friends, or family or charge it.
39	When I shop for something I want, I will spend my bill money.

SECTION V : SHOPPING – WANTS

40	When I shop for something I want, I shop around for the best price, or a sale or use coupons
41	When I shop for something I want, I purchase it on the spot.

SECTION VI : SHOPPING – NEEDS

42	When I shop for something I need, I wait until I have enough to pay for it
43	When I shop for something I need and don't have enough to purchase it, I borrow the additional funds from friends, or family or charge it.
44	When I shop for something I need, I will spend my bill money.

SECTION VII : SHOPPING – NEEDS

45	When I shop for something I need, I shop around for the best price, or a sale or use coupons
46	When I shop for something I need, I purchase it on the spot.

POINT VALUES

Now that you've completed answering the previous questions, you need to determine your score. Each section has one answer, so you can see what you scored by assigning the corresponding point value below. When all seven section scores are added together, the total score should not exceed 50.

SECTION I : GIVING

Based on your choice on page 16, you are going to determine how many points you've scored by the choice you made. For example, If you chose #3, you scored 10 points, which you can write in the second column provided.

#1: Point Value	3	
#2: Point Value	0	
#3: Point Value	10	
#4: Point Value	3	
GIVING SECTION SCORE		

SECTION II : SPENDING

Based on your choice on pages 16-17, locate your score and write it in the second column.

#5: Point Value	0	
#6: Point Value	5	
#7: Point Value	0	
#8: Point Value	5	
#9: Point Value	5	
#10: Point Value	3	

#11: Point Value	7	
#12: Point Value	5	
#13: Point Value	7	
#14: Point Value	3	
#15: Point Value	10	
#16: Point Value	10	
#17: Point Value	10	
#18: Point Value	3	
#19: Point Value	10	
#20: Point Value	7	
#21: Point Value	10	
#22: Point Value	3	
#23: Point Value	10	
#24: Point Value	7	
#25: Point Value	10	
#26: Point Value	10	
#27: Point Value	5	
#28: Point Value	3	
#29: Point Value	0	
SPENDING SECTION SCORE		

SECTION III : SAVING / INVESTING

Based on your choice on page 18, locate your score and write it in the second column.

#30: Point Value	5	
#31: Point Value	7	
#32: Point Value	3	
#33: Point Value	0	
#34: Point Value	7	

#35: Point Value	10	
#36: Point Value	7	
SAVING / INVESTING SECTION SCORE		

SECTION IV : SHOPPING – WANTS

Based on your choice on page 19, locate your score and write it in the second column.

#37: Point Value	5	
#38: Point Value	2	
#39: Point Value	0	
SHOPPING – WANTS SECTION SCORE		

SECTION V : SHOPPING – WANTS

Based on your choice on page 19, locate your score and write it in the second column.

#40: Point Value	5	
#41: Point Value	2	
SHOPPING – WANTS SECTION SCORE		

SECTION VI : SHOPPING – NEEDS

Based on your choice on page 19, locate your score and write it in the second column.

#42: Point Value	2	
#43: Point Value	5	
#44: Point Value	1	
SHOPPING – NEEDS SECTION SCORE		

SECTION VII : SHOPPING – NEEDS

Based on your choice on page 19, locate your score and write it in the second column.

#45: Point Value	5	
#46: Point Value	3	
SHOPPING – NEEDS SECTION SCORE		

TOTAL POINTS :

Calculate your total points by adding all the section scores together.

TOTAL SCORE		

OBSERVATIONS:

This section provides rationale for the points assigned to each option.

SECTION I: GIVING

As a Christian giving is at the core of who we are and what we do. Faithful giving is rated the highest (10 points – Option #3). As a Christian not giving is rated 0 (Option #2). Options #1 and #4 shows occasional attempts at giving and is assigned 3 points for being on the pathway to faithful giving.

SECTION II: SPENDING

Options #15, #16, #17, #19, #21, #23, #25 and #26 shows balance in spending and are equally weighted at 10 points. Needs and wants were addressed and some bills were paid.(if applicable). Remember this is extra money which could help you get ahead. So if there were still some things that were needed by all means use the extra blessing to purchase them. Extra funds are also the perfect time to splurge. Treat yourself, after all you work hard! When possible we should also take advantage of paying down our bills. Great job to all who selected one of these options!

Options   #11, #13, #20 and #24 were pretty good and were weighted 7 points. Options #11, #20, and #24 were no fun. Option #11 and #24 address needs only.   In Option #11 no wants were identified and no bills were paid. In #24, there were no bills. However both seem to have been selected out of necessity, leaving no room for bills and/or wants.   Any option where needs are selected is the responsible thing to do. However, this may point to underlying problems. Either spending in our regular budget should be reduced or more income is needed. In Option #20 needs were addressed, some bills were paid but none of the wants were purchased.   As stated earlier, when extra funds show up that are outside of our regular income, we should consider treating ourselves, even if it is something small. Option #13 addressed needs and wants; however no bills were paid. Perhaps more balance could have been given on the wants that were purchased to allow some funds to be allocated to bills.

Options #6, #8, #9, #12 and #27 were assigned 5 points. Under each option, needs were addressed. Option #6 no bills were paid but things that were wanted were not purchased. This was a missed opportunity on two fronts – bill payment and getting what was wanted. In Option #8, there was nothing needed or wanted, bills could have been addressed. In Option #9, everything was spent on wants but no bills were paid. There were no needs at the time. While splurging is encouraged when unexpected funds are received, we must keep in mind that this is a one- time gift and paying on bills is a future gift to ourselves. In #12, no bills were paid nor were any wants addressed. (Refer to the explanations for #20 above under 7 points.) Under Option #27, there were no bills and nothing was needed; however none of the wants were purchased.

Options #10, #14, #18, #22, and #28 had one thing in common that led to a rating of 3. This was an opportunity to address needs. Needs were left on the table unmet.

Options #5, #7 and #29 were rated 0. Under Options #5 and #7, nothing was purchased, no bills were paid and needs were not met. In addition, under Option #7, things that were wanted were not purchased. Under Option #29, in addition to not having any bills, no purchases were made. Needs and wants were unmet. This was a unique position to be in and the opportunities Options #29 presented were lost.

SECTION III: SAVING/INVESTING

Option #35 is the ideal position to be in. Emergency funds are on hand and focus is on long term financial goals. This option was awarded 10 points.

Options #31, #34 and #36 are worth 7 points each. We should take into account emergencies first and then long- term financial needs. Option #31 indicates that savings is a constant goal. Option #34 shows that funds were split between emergency needs and long- term goals. The issue with Option #34, is that if an emergency arises before reaching the long- term goal, the funds set aside for long- term goals will be reduced to help meet the emergency. Option #36 has the same challenges as Option #34 Keep in mind even if you have provided emergency funds, an emergency could always exceed what was saved and eat into your long-term funds.

Option #30 is worth 5 points. Savings is something that is being attempted. Funds were set aside for emergency purposes.

Option #33, to never save is indicative of several issues and is rated 0. Our desires could be high and we cannot defer gratification. Or bills are so high, nothing can be saved right now. Or our attitude is such that tomorrow is not promised, so why save. I am sure other reasons can be added to this list.

SECTIONS IV, V, VI & VII :

SHOPPING FOR WANTS AND NEEDS

Sections IV and V which deals with shopping for wants and Sections VI and VII which deals with shopping for needs will be discussed together.

Whether you are shopping for wants or needs it is always good to do price comparisons to try to get the best possible deal, thus a rating of 5 was awarded for Options #40 and #45 which are excellent choices. To save for a want is wonderful and shows self-discipline. A word of caution, time may be a factor in purchasing a need, and we may or may not have enough time to shop for good prices. Option #37 is worthy of 5 points. To save for a need may not be the way to go depending on the need and the timing.

Option #42 was awarded only 2 points. We should never borrow for wants and should only charge if the item can be paid for before interest is assessed to the account. Option #38 was weighted 2 points. Sometimes a need could be an emergency situation which may require you to charge for the item or borrow funds. 5 points was awarded for selecting Option #43. To spend your bill money on something you want is unwise. Always take care of business first. Option #39 was awarded 0 points. Likewise with needs you may decide to spend bill money. If this occurs your options should be weighed carefully. This indicates that your overall finances are in trouble. However, we must do what is needed to take care of ourselves and family, for that reason Option #44 is awarded 1 point. When you purchase something you want on the spot, not bad if it is one of a kind or the only one left. However, if you have the opportunity to shop around, take it. Option #41 is awarded 2 points. Finally buying what you need on the spot could indicate that there is a timing factor associated with meeting the need and there may be no time or limited time in doing your due diligence. Do what you have to. Option #46 is awarded 3 points.

RATINGS:

45 – 50	Way to Go
40 – 44	Almost There
35 – 39	Keep Going
30 – 34	Don't Fool Yourself – You Can Do This
29 & Below	Roll Up Your Sleeves & Let's Get to Work NOW

This brief exercise incorporated several aspects of a healthy budget: Giving, Spending, Prioritizing Needs vs Wants, Smart Shopping and Saving. All of these topics from a biblical perspective will be covered at length in the following pages. It is my desire that something helpful is shared that you can incorporate into your financial lifestyle.

STEWARDSHIP

The silver is mine, and the gold is mine saith the Lord of hosts

Haggai 2:8

Why is it so important for a Christian to handle their resources responsibly? In the beginning, God entrusted man to have power or control over every living creature as we can see from the following verses:

28 And God blessed them, and God said unto them, Be fruitful, and multiply, and replenish the earth, and subdue it: and have dominion over the fish of the sea, and over the fowl of the air, and over every living thing that moveth upon the earth.

29 And God said, Behold, I have given you every herb bearing seed, which is upon the face of all the earth, and every tree, in the which is the fruit of a tree yielding seed; to you it shall be for meat.'

Genesis 1:28-29

God created the Garden of Eden and placed man as a caretaker.

And the Lord God took the man, and put him into the garden of Eden to dress it and to keep it.' Genesis 2:15

Man entered this world with nothing and will leave with nothing. Every resource man has during his life, whether it be finances, material things, animals, plants, etc., comes from God and is given to man as God's steward or caretaker.

> The earth is the Lord's, and the fullness thereof; the world and they that dwell therein. Psalm 24:1

Thus, there is a need for a discussion on stewardship as it relates to our finances.

According to Merriam-Webster, stewardship is a steward's office, duties, and obligations. The conducting, supervising, or managing of something, especially the careful and responsible management of something entrusted to one's care.' God has provided our resources or blessings. It is expected of each believer to use resources provided to them godly and wisely. We are God's stewards, and the resources under our care should advance the kingdom of God. What does this mean? After providing the Lord with His tithes and offerings, we should ensure the care of those entrusted to us – our families.

The scripture tells us that:

> But if any provide not for his own, and specially for those of his own house, he hath denied the faith and is worse than an infidel.
>
> I Timothy 5:8

Beyond this, we should extend a helping hand, when possible, to our neighbor. We know from studying the parable of the Good Samaritan (Luke 10:29-37) that anyone we encounter is our neighbor.

Let's look more closely at stewardship from God's perspective. Consider: Matthew 25:14-30

14 For the kingdom of heaven is as a man travelling into a far country, who called his own servants, and delivered unto them his goods.

15 And unto one he gave five talents, to another two, and to another one; to every man according to his several ability; and straightway took his journey.

16 Then he that had received the five talents went and traded with the same, and made them other five talents.

17 And like-wise he that had received two, he also gained other two.

18 But he that had received one went and digged in the earth, and hid his Lord's money.

19 After a long time the Lord of those servants cometh, and reckoneth with them.

20 And so he that had received five talents came and brought other five talents, saying Lord, thou deliveredst unto me five talents: behold, I have gained beside them five talents more.

21 His Lord said unto him, Well done, thou good and faithful servant: thou hast been faithful

over a few things, I will make thee ruler over many things: enter thou into the joy of the Lord.

22 He also that had received two talents came and said, Lord, thou deliveredst unto me two talents: behold, I have gained two other talents beside them.

23 His Lord said unto him, Well done, good and faithful servant; thou hast been faithful over a few things, I will make thee ruler over many things; enter thou into the joy of the Lord.

24 Then he which had received the one talent came and said, Lord, I knew thee that thou art an hard man, reaping where thou hast not sown, and gathering where thou hast not strawed:

25 And I was afraid, and went and hid thy talent in the earth: lo, there thou hast that is thine.

26 His Lord answered and said unto him, Thou wicked and slothful servant, thou knewest that I reap where I sowed not, and gather where I have not strawed:

27 Thou oughtest therefore to have put my money to the exchangers, and then at my coming I should have received mine own

with usury.

28 Take therefore the talent from him, and give it unto him which hath ten talents.

29 For unto every one that hath shall be given, and he shall have abundance; but from him that hath not shall be taken away even that which he hath.

30 And cast ye the unprofitable servant into outer darkness: there shall be weeping and gnashing of teeth.

The above scripture is a parable. Telling parables was one of Christ's teaching methods. It is an earthly story that the people of the day could relate to that guides them to a spiritual understanding. In this parable, the man represents Christ. The journey is Christ's going away and one day returning to earth. The entrustment of talents represents the gifts and resources that Christ has blessed everyone with. The man's return and the rewards and punishments being meted out represent what happens on judgment day. God's good and faithful servants are rewarded on that day, and those who were not wise stewards were banished to eternity in hell.

The scripture shares how God views the things He has entrusted us with. Doing nothing with your talents and blessings causes God to consider you wicked and slothful. (Slothful in this context means lazy.) He gives good and perfect gifts to everyone according to His good measure. He gives you what He knows you can handle, and to do nothing with it causes an eternal separation from Him. Your failure to believe and have faith that the Lord will return and hold you accountable will be the reason. At that time, every knee shall bow, and every tongue shall confess.

We can see at least seven principles of stewardship that evolve from this parable:

1. God owns everything. (As represented by the man who gave the talents to each servant.)

2. The people of God are God's management team (As seen by the relationship between the man and the servants)

3. Accountability is a critical part of stewardship. (In the meeting held with each servant, the servant was held accountable for the talents under his management.)

4. A commitment to another is required. (Just like the servants had an obligation to manage talents, we also have a commitment to God to manage gifts/blessings/etc which He entrusts to us.)

5. Stewardship carries eternal consequences. (The man separated himself from the servant who did nothing with his talents. Likewise, what we do with gifts, blessings, etc., that God gives us will determine our eternal consequences.)

6. The rewards tied to stewardship are based not only on accountability but also on capability. Two servants received praise and rewards. The rewards were not based on the number of talents the servants were entrusted with. One received more talents than the other, but the eternal consequences for both were the same.

7. Finally, we must know our master. If we know in advance that our mishandling of God's gifts would cause separation from Him, would we change how we use them for His glory?

God knows your ability, so it does not matter whether He gives you a little or plenty. It does not matter what talents or the amount of talent He blesses you with. The reward for using whatever He blesses you with is great. It is the ultimate - living in eternity with Him. He knows what you are capable of, so excuses with how little you think you can and cannot do are unfounded in His sight.

As we continue through God's Bailout Plan, ask yourself these questions:

Am I using God's financial resources wisely?

Did I do what God expects of me with the finances He has blessed me with?

Have I been lazy or selfish with God's resources?

Should I change my lifestyle that is supported by my spending to align it with God's will for my life? (i.e., this includes wasteful spending.)

Am I taking care of my family the way I should?

When my neighbor needs help, do I take the time to do what I can, whether it is financial or requires a little time?

Do I have enough faith in the Lord to follow His Bailout Plan?

> He that is faithful in that which is least is faithful also in much: and he that is unjust in the least is unjust also in much
>
> Luke 16:10

FINANCIAL PITFALLS

Take heed, and beware of covetousness: for a man's life consisteth not in the abundance of the things which he possesseth.

Luke 12:15

Let's spend a few moments discussing our attitude towards money. A person's attitude towards money will affect/determine one's relationship with God. God calls for balance in our lives and complete trust in Him in every aspect, including our finances.

Your attitude or feelings about money will also determine your financial outlook which drives your decisions. For example, If you are stingy, you will keep your money close. Sharing/giving is little to none, long delays are experienced in replacing or acquiring needed items, food is being stretched unreasonably, etc. Have you ever heard the expression that nothing can get in or out of a closed fist? Holding your money tight does not let you share, nor does keeping a closed fist let blessings flow in.

If you are a spendthrift, you may always be buying something. Bills may get paid late or not at all, some necessities may not be provided, you may be a hoarder, etc.

Most of us fall somewhere between stingy and spendthrift.

An individual's attitude towards money is so essential that many verses and stories in the bible are devoted to money and material possessions. Jesus taught thirty-eight parables, sixteen of which dealt with money—over 2,000 verses in the bible address this topic. If the bible warns and guides us on this subject, we should take heed of the pitfalls and warnings taught.

We will review financial pitfalls to understand more clearly how our attitude toward money impacts our financial decisions.

PITFALLS OF THE WEALTHY

There is nothing wrong with being wealthy. There are several examples in the bible of rich men, such as Job, Abraham, David, Solomon, etc., who loved the Lord. The problem occurs when trust is placed in the money and ourselves. The feelings of self-dependency replace our love and dependency on the Lord.

SCRIPTURAL WARNINGS ABOUT WEALTH / MONEY: Remember that these warnings apply not only to the wealthy. Many are not wealthy but fall into some of these pitfalls.

He that loveth silver shall not be satisfied with silver; nor he that loveth abundance with increase: this is also vanity.

Ecclesiastes 5:10

For the love of money is the root of all evil: which while some coveted after, they have erred from the faith, and pierced themselves through with many sorrows.

1 Timothy 6:10

And the cares of this world, and the deceitfulness of riches, and the lusts of other things entering in, choke the word, and it becometh unfruitful.

Mark 4: 19

He that trusteth in his riches shall fall: but the righteous shall flourish as a branch

Proverbs 11:28

Riches profit not in the day of wrath: but righteousness delivereth from death.

Proverbs 11:4

Labor not to be rich: cease from thine own wisdom.

Proverbs 23:4

For what shall it profit a man, if he shall gain the whole world, and lose his own soul?

Mark 8:36

Jesus provides us with an illustration of the pitfalls of wealth in Luke 12:16 – 21.

16 And he spake a parable unto them, saying, The ground of a certain rich man brought forth plentifully:

17 And he thought within himself, saying, What shall I do, because I have no room where to bestow my fruits?

18 And he said, This will I do: I will pull down my barns, and build greater; and there will I bestow all my fruits and my goods.

19 And I will say to my soul, Soul, thou hast much goods laid up for many years; take thine ease, eat, drink, and be merry.

20 But God said unto him, Thou fool, this night thy soul shall be required of thee: then whose shall those things be which thou has provided?

21 So is he that layeth up treasure for himself, and is not rich toward God.

Luke 12:16 – 21

The problem in this parable is that God had blessed the rich man incredibly; however the rich man showed no signs of gratitude toward the giver. Additionally, he gave no thought to others who may not have fared as well as he. Subsequently, he planned to go to great expense to keep all he had. Finally, he planned to do nothing but pleasure himself while he enjoyed the fruits of his labor. God wants you to depend on Him and not what you think are your capabilities or resources. As long as we feel it is our doing, it is our money, it is our ... there is no room to thank God or to depend on Him. Sadly, the rich man could not carry out his plans. The results of his hard labor would go to someone else. How different would the outcome for the rich man be if he had shown some balance with his blessings and not kept them all for himself?

THE ADVICE THE LORD HAS FOR THE WEALTHY:

17 Charge them that are rich in this world, that they be not highminded, nor trust in uncertain riches, but in the living God, who giveth us richly all things to enjoy.

18 That they do good works, ready to distribute, willing to communicate;

19 Laying up in store for themselves a good foundation against the time to come, that they may lay hold on eternal life.'

I Timothy 6:17 – 19

Remember: 'It is easier for a camel to go through the eye of a needle, than for a rich man to enter into the kingdom of God.'

Mark 10:25

PITFALLS THAT LEAD TO POVERTY

Just as there are pitfalls for the wealthy, there are also things we can do that will bring about poverty, such as slothfulness, laziness, overindulgence, pleasure-seeking, and covetousness.

SLOTHFULNESS/LAZINESS

We all know people who may be disabled and cannot work or what they can do is limited. In those cases, we are to help them. However, if an individual can work, then his charge is to provide food for himself and his household.

For even when we were with you, this we commanded you, that is any would not work, neither should he eat.

2 Thessalonians 3:10

He becometh poor that dealeth with a slack hand: but the hand of the diligent maketh rich.

Proverbs 10:4

OVERINDULGENCE

For the drunkard and the glutton shall come to Poverty: and drowsiness shall clothe a man with rags.

Proverbs 23:21

Excess drinking impacts work performance, relationships, ability to drive safely, think clearly, etc. Alcoholism destroys families.

Likewise, gluttony, or overeating, is harmful to the body. Eventually, it causes obesity, leading to many health issues. Finally, such actions lead to a loss of income. A loss of income leads to poverty. Drunkenness and overeating lead to drowsiness. If we are eating, drinking, and sleeping excessively, the result is devastating to our ability to earn a living.

'Love not sleep, lest thou come to poverty; open thine eyes, and thou shalt be satisfied with bread.'

Proverbs 20:13

PLEASURE SEEKING

Almost any activity we engage in can become habitual. We could watch too much television, play too many electronic games, surf the internet for hours on end, drink too much, overeat, sleep too much, sex addictions, food addictions, etc. Because of the rise in addictions, support organizations have emerged to address some of these addictions, such as Alcoholics Anonymous, Gamblers Anonymous, etc. Many of these activities begin innocently, and some are a part of most individual's life at some point. However, carrying them to extreme interferes with the time we need to work, care for our family, etc. When it gets to where it consumes most of our day, our jobs/careers are in danger, and poverty is just around the corner.

He that loveth pleasure shall be a poor man: he that loveth wine and oil shall not be rich.'

Proverbs 21:17

COVETOUSNESS

Covetous is marked by an inordinate desire for wealth or possessions or another's possessions. (Source: Merriam-Webster) This desire to keep up with the 'Joneses' has led many to financial ruin. The Lord felt so strongly about this desire that He warned us against it in the Ten Commandments. He also wants us to know to:

… Take heed, and beware of covetousness: for a man's life consisteth not in the abundance of the things which he possesseth.'

Luke 12:15

The rest of this book guides a healthy and balanced financial life. Set aside any bad habits that led you to where you are and open your hearts and minds to being a good steward and managing your finances in a way that is pleasing to Christ.

For where your treasure is, there will your heart be also.' Luke 12:34

GIVING

And all the tithe of the land, whether of the seed of the land, or the fruit of the tree, is the Lord's: it is holy unto the Lord.

Leviticus 27:30

At the crux of Christianity is charity (love). To be charitable (Which is loving), you must give. You cannot love someone if you do nothing for them. If needed, a loved one will occasionally receive some of your time, gifts, and financial resources. Love for God is shown in two ways:

1) How you love and respect Him and
2) How you treat and love others.

So then, how can you say you love the Lord yet never or seldom give? God wants your resources so that kingdom-building is supported. The purpose of the church is to have resources so the needs of others can be met, whether it is to feed the hungry, spread and teach the gospel, clothe the naked, provide housing for the homeless, etc. Without the gifts of the parishioners, none of this work can go forth from the church.

Giving for the Christian is not limited to the church or to loved ones; your neighbor may need support. A child or children attending school may need some help. You do not have to give away your bill money or life savings. You are expected to do what you can do when you can. However, the Lord has included specifics on when, what, where, and how to give to His church. You can use your judgment to help outside of the church environment.

WHEN TO GIVE

Proverbs 3:9 states: Honor the Lord with your wealth and the first fruits of all your produce. During this period of human history, man lived in an agrarian society. Many had farmlands and animals. Their wealth was reflected in the quantity of these possessions. The first fruits then were the first produce and the best of the harvest season. When animals were sacrificed, they were not ill or deformed but perfect. These offerings did not represent what was leftover, misshapen or decayed. It was given off the top. This showed reverence, gratefulness and respect to the giver of the blessings.

Today, the economy is diverse, and individuals make their living from many industries outside of farming. An application of first fruits is to give to the Lord before any other spending occurs. This may be difficult to do because most paydays do not align with worship days. So, how can we honor God by giving to Him first? Deduct your church donations from your income before paying any bills. Whatever remains is used to pay bills, save, etc. Donations are paid at the very first worship service following payday. With electronic options, we can more closely honor this principle by paying our donations on the same day as our payday.

What is key is to give to the Lord every time He gives to you!

WHAT TO GIVE

Malachi 3:8-10 lays out some guidelines, curses, and promises for giving.

8 Will a man rob God? Yet ye have robbed me.
   But ye say, Wherein have we robbed thee?
   In tithes and offerings.

9 Ye are cursed with a curse: for ye have robbed me, even this whole nation.

10 Bring ye all the tithes into the storehouse, that there may be meat in mine house, and prove me now herewith, saith the Lord of hosts, if I will not open you the windows of heaven, and pour you out a blessing, that there shall not be room enough to receive it.

Malachi 3:8-10

Many may ask if tithing was done away within the New Testament since it is not mentioned by name. No, it was not.

Woe unto you, scribes and Pharisees, hypocrites! For ye pay tithe of mint and anise and cumin, and have omitted the weightier matters of the law, judgment, mercy, and faith: these ought ye have done, and not leave the other undone.

Matthew 23:23

Here, Jesus points out that there are some things weightier or more important than tithing; however, He did not mean they should tend to the weightier matters and leave giving undone.

The tithe. What, then is a tithe? A tithe is ten percent of your earnings. This is your earnings times 10% or your earnings divided by 10. For example, If you make $200 a week, then your tithes for that week are $20 ($200 times 10%).

A follow-up question I often receive is: Should I tithe off of my gross or net earnings? When you receive a job offer in the United States, your employer always makes the offer based on the gross amount. For example, you might be offered $1,000 per week but only receive $800. What happened to the difference between the $1,000 offered and the $800 received? The employer must take federal income taxes, any applicable state or county income taxes, and FICA (Federal Insurance Contributions Act) tax. The FICA funds support the U.S. Social Security Program for retired and disabled citizens.

There may also be other deductions, such as the employee's share of employer-sponsored health care plans, pension plans, thrift plans, etc. The mandatory taxes that the employer takes out of one's earning is required by law. These are expenses paid on your behalf to federal, state, and local governments that represent your financial obligations as a citizen of the United States and your state.

The answer would be gross when you look at the question posed from this direction.

The offering. Offerings are up to you. In the Baptist church, there are many opportunities and occasions for offerings as the education department (or Sunday School), special building projects, various outreach ministries, etc. Or if you are a church that has streamlined giving, then the tithes would be 10%, and an additional amount would be added for the offering.

The robber. There is a difference between a thief and a robber. The thief waits until no one is watching and steals the items of interest. The robber is bolder. They will steal in your presence. (examples: carjacker, purse snatcher, bank and armed robbery, etc.) The sad part about robbing God is that He knows exactly how much you have kept from Him because you did it in His presence.

God's Curses. God's curses are not identified in the verses shared; however, no one wants to be on the end of whatever that is!

God's Blessings. Finally, He promises to open the windows of heaven to pour out blessings too large to receive. Have you ever noticed, as you walk from room to room, that if all the glass from your windows and all the doors were removed from their hinges, more could enter the windows than the doors? God is not specific about what blessings He will pour your way, but whether it is good health, good friends, healthy family members, or, yes, financial gifts, wouldn't you want to try Him and see what happens? Because that is exactly what He is inviting you/challenging you to do.

WHERE TO GIVE

Your local church is the perfect place to give. However, some may not be members of a church for various reasons. Your options are to give to the previous church where you held your membership or get recommendations from friends or family members of a church so you can send your tithes and offerings to them until you can find a church home.

I have also been asked if giving your tithes and offerings to a charitable organization is okay. There is nothing wrong with supporting a charitable organization, but it is not the organization God had in mind when He said to bring the tithe to His storehouse. It would help if you remembered that not every charitable organization is faith-based. Some charitable organizations have a high overhead, and the funds collected go more towards administrative costs than the established cause. So, contribute to charitable organizations you consider worthy, but not at the expense of the Lord's house.

HOW TO GIVE

CHEERFULLY

> Every man according as he purposeth in his heart, so let him give; not grudgingly, or of necessity: for God loveth a cheerful giver.
>
> 2 Corinthians 9:7

The Lord is concerned about the heart. Have you ever asked your children or spouse to do something, and their attitude was horrible? How did you feel? Depending on what it was, you would rather not accept it. That's the same with God. He doesn't want you to give because you want something in return (of necessity) or grudgingly (you really would rather not give). He wants you to give freely because you love Him and cheerfully wish to show your gratitude.

REGULARLY

> On the first day of the week, let every one of you lay by him in store, as God hath prospered him, that there be no gatherings when I come. 1 Corinthians 16:2

In this verse, Paul collected donations for the persecuted Christians in Jerusalem. He encouraged the church in Corinth to set aside money every week according to what they had. This is a reference to giving within your means. Wealthy people would be expected to provide more because they had more, and the poor would give less. However, everyone was urged to give every week until Paul could return to collect the funds. You cannot give every week if you do not have money coming in every week. So give when God has blessed you with financial resources.

GENEROUSLY

In these two verses, Paul speaks about generosity. 1) For I testify that they gave as much as they were able, and even beyond their ability.' 2 Corinthians 8:3 'Whoever sows sparingly will also reap sparingly, and whoever sows generously will also reap generously'. 2 Corinthians 9:6

One of the greatest stories about generosity comes from Luke 21:1-4.

1   And he looked up, and saw the rich men casting their gifts into the treasury.

2   And he saw also a certain poor widow casting in thither two mites.

3   And he said, Of a truth I say unto you, that this poor widow hath cast in more than they all:

4   For all these have of their abundance cast in unto the offerings of God: but she of her penury hath cast in all the living that she had.

Verse 1, the reader may form the impression that Jesus was impressed with what the rich men were doing. By verse 3, however, we see that the widow's offerings impressed Jesus. Why? She placed two mites in the treasury. During New Testament times, a mite was worth 1/64 of a denarius. A denarius was a day's wage for the typical worker. The value in U.S. currency is 1/8 of a cent. She gave two mites, so the value of her offering was 2/8 of a cent. This offering was small, especially compared to the amount the wealthy placed in the treasury. The answer to how Jesus felt lies in verse 4. The widow gave all the living she had. All means 100%. Compared to the wealthy, the percentage they were giving was far less. The heart and the sacrifice impresses the Lord and not the amount. The widow's gift was the most generous gift of the day.

...give, and it shall be given unto you; good measure, pressed down, and shaken together, and running over, shall men give into your bosom. For with the same measure that ye mete withal it shall be measured to you again.

Luke 6:38

SPENDING PART I: PURCHASE WHAT YOU CAN AFFORD

For which of you, intending to build a tower, does not sit down first and count the cost, whether he has enough to finish it?

Luke 14:28

We are bombarded with commercials to buy, buy, buy. Even talk shows, such as The Talk and The View, feature products that can be purchased at 'great deals' if you buy them within a limited timeframe. There are frequent upgrades to electronics. Electronics bought today are obsolete within months after they are purchased.

Banking apps and debit cards have made buying so convenient. Credit card companies offer rewards. The more you spend, the greater the rewards. Many products purchased from Amazon can be delivered the next day. There is pressure from all sides to spend, spend, spend.

There is more self-control in our spending when the price tag is significant. When we buy a home, for example, the mortgage company takes very stringent steps to make sure you are a good bet. Mortgage companies will determine the maximum amount approved for home loans. But when you hold several credit cards and they all are in play, you could lose sight of how much is being spent and what the resulting minimum payments will be. You may reach the point where excess spending across several cards renders you unable to meet minimum payments. This level of credit card spending is an extreme but realistic example of an individual not spending within affordable levels.

Prayerfully, this spending section will help bring spending patterns under control. Even if only one suggestion can be implemented, do it consistently to maximize the benefit.

Spending has been divided into two sections: Purchase What You Can Afford and Pay What You Owe.

He that loveth silver shall not be satisfied with silver; nor he that loveth abundance with increase: this is also vanity.

Ecclesiastes 5:10

NEEDS VERSUS WANTS

But my God shall supply all your need according to his riches in glory by Christ Jesus.

Philippians 4:19

DISTINGUISH BETWEEN NEEDS AND WANTS

The determination of needs and wants will differ from individual to individual. However, there are basic similarities in our needs. For example, common needs include food, water, shelter, clothing, and medical necessities. A need is something an individual requires to survive. Wants are things that are desirable but are not required for your survival. When looking at what is affordable, consider first the need. If you have a choice between buying food versus a handbag, buying food wins out. Wants are not being downplayed. We all have desires and it is good to have what we want; however, we should never sacrifice our needs over our wants.

FOCUS ON NEEDS FIRST

Needed items may require prioritization. Naturally, rent should be paid if we must decide between clothing and rent. We can always patch up clothing one more time. Each time a paycheck or other forms of income is received, focus on what is necessary between this paycheck and the next. If there isn't enough to provide for the household's needs, consider these options:

1. Determine if you are obtaining goods and services at the most affordable prices.

2. Acquire more income. Determine how much more income is needed and find part-time employment to supplement your paycheck.

3. Review your spending habits and identify any areas that can be reduced.

4. Improve your skillsets by taking courses that will help you to increase your income. This option takes longer than the other options. However, this may eliminate the need for part-time employment in the long run.

FOCUS ON WANTS LAST

Depending on how much of your income is spent on needs, you may have to save to provide for your wants. If several items are wanted, focus on them according to their importance. You could prioritize by cost, with the least expensive first and the costliest item last, or you could do the opposite: save for the most expensive item first and the least expensive item last. If there are multiple wants within the household between parents and children, sit down as a family and decide the order in which wants will be provided.

...casting all your care upon him; for he careth for you

I Peter 5:7

STRETCH THAT DOLLAR

...Gather up the fragments that remain, that nothing be lost

John 6:12

The above scripture is insightful into Jesus' teachings about waste. Jesus fed over 5,000 people with two fish and five loaves of bread. After everyone had eaten as much as they wanted, Jesus instructed his disciples to gather the leftovers. Jesus, who could provide such an abundance, was interested in the 12 baskets of leftover food. Not that he could not produce more. Of course, he could. However, the leftovers were just as good as the initial servings. The scripture did not say what was done with the bread. So what does this tell us? We want to use God's blessings wisely. Leftovers are to be put to good use instead of being thrown away. If you can buy something at a lower cost, then stretch that dollar and use the leftover money for other needs or wants. The less you waste, the more you'll have for other things. This section includes references to several apps and practices that can save money.

COUPONS

There are browser extensions for online shopping. A browser extension is software that adds features to your web browser or to programs you use in your browser. For example, the Honey app, one of the most popular browser extensions, automatically finds and applies coupon codes at checkout with a single click. It is free and has a massive database.

Four other browser extensions for online shopping are:

Rakuten Cash Back Button earns cash back.
Giving Assistant earns cash back and provides coupons.
The Camelizer by CamelCamelCamel tracks historical Amazon prices and sets up watches for price drops.
The Invisible Hand provides the lowest pricing on shopping flights, hotels, and rental cars. It also includes information on lower prices offered elsewhere.

There are more than five browser extensions. This is only a partial list. Most function similarly but have their own nuisances. Some are better at finding deals on clothes rather than electronics. You may use a couple of them to get a nice balance. A word of caution: These apps exist to stimulate shopping. Remember that your goal is to make your purchases more affordable and not be tempted to spend more.

You may also follow your favorite brands on social media. For example, by following your brand of interest on Instagram, you may receive a coupon or announcements on early releases of upcoming products.

Clipping coupons take work. They may be found in magazines or newspapers. Many vendors will email coupons to you. Find out from your favorite stores which ones will email coupons and begin receiving them right away.

REWARD PROGRAMS

Many fast-food restaurants, gas stations, credit cards, etc., offer reward programs. You may have to download an app, swipe your rewards card, or use a particular credit card for purchases. When purchases are made, the purchase is recorded, and your reward points are updated. You may track your points and search the app for rewards you may qualify for. Sixty-one rewards programs are described at https://moneypantry.com/rewards-programs. Visit the site, determine if any favorite stores are listed, and enroll at your earliest convenience.

There are reward apps where you can earn gift cards, sweepstake entries, and/or cash back. They require copies of receipts to be scanned, and each receipt is awarded points. After you have collected enough points, you can then select a reward. Such apps include Fetch Rewards, Ibotta, Swagbucks, Rakuten, Caddle, SavingStar, ReceiptPal, and Receipt Hog. This is not a complete listing of programs. These apps require copies of your receipts. There are no fees or additional costs to you, just a little time. The gift cards can come in handy for gifts to others or buying things you may want. It is worth looking into!

BRAND NAMES VERSUS GENERIC

Like many suggestions provided, it comes down to personal preference. You can go down any aisle in the grocery store and compare name brands to generic brands. The noticeable difference is cost. Brand names cost from 30 cents to $5 more than their generic counterpart. Because of this considerable price variance, conduct a taste test between the brand name you've been buying versus its generic counterpart. If you cannot tell the difference in the performance or taste of a product, consider the less expensive item. For example, I cannot tell the difference in the taste of table salt. So, choosing between a brand named salt and a generic brand, I would choose the generic. However, I tried the same thing with garlic powder. The generic brand required large quantities to season food properly, so I stick with brand names. If you are equally pleased, choose the generic for the savings. If you cannot bring yourself to try the generic brand, then stick with the brand-name product. This is, of course, if you can afford it.

PRICE COMPARISONS

Generally, several stores offer the same products. Find out which stores carry what you are interested in buying and the price. Consider buying the item for the lowest price. This takes some work. However, there are apps to help with this as well. ShopSavvy and Amazinger are just two of the apps that can assist you with locating an item for the lowest price. The apps may search in different ways. Amazinger searches Amazon sites, but ShopSavvy compares prices at different stores. Determine the best bar scanner app for you and conserve your energy and gas.

SALES

When shopping, especially for major items such as cars, furniture, appliances, etc. Consider purchasing these items around the holidays. There is usually a Memorial Day Sale, Fourth of July sale, Labor Day Sale, Black Friday, Ciber Monday, etc. Also look at clearance items. If you don't mind last year's model or a dent, consider the savings and acquire the clearance item. Don't do it if you cannot live with the dent, scratch, etc. Always walk away pleased with your purchase.

DEFERRED INTEREST PROGRAMS OR SAME AS CASH

Most vendors of major items, such as furniture, appliances, etc., will offer in-store credit cards that may offer same as cash or deferred interest programs. The offers vary, but let's say you are buying furniture and are offered an 18-month interest-free payment plan. Divide the total purchase cost by 18 and see if you can afford the monthly bill. Remember, if you do not pay the bill on time and/or do not make the payment in full at the end of the 18 months, then the cost of the deferred interest will be added to your bill.

SUBSCRIPTIONS

Subscriptions are another way of saving money. Seek subscription deals for your favorite magazines or newspapers. If you are an avid reader, you might subscribe to such apps as Audible. There are also subscription boxes for repeat purchases you may subscribe to. Again, homework is needed here to determine if you are saving by subscribing or if it is a matter of convenience.

BARTER SYSTEM

We live in a great community and have been able to use the barter system, if only in a limited sense. During the winter, my neighbor would plow our driveway. In return, we would take care of his family's computer issues. In my mom's neighborhood, a neighbor uses her snowblower to clear her walkways and driveway during the winter and in return, he uses the snowblower to clear his own. Find ways that this will work with family, friends or neighbors.

INSURANCE

Accidents, illnesses, home robberies, death, etc., always carry unexpected expenses. If you cannot afford to pay for damages associated with a car accident or replace or rebuild your home in case of fire or natural disaster, etc., consider insurance.

Car Insurance

Shop around for prices on full coverage. If your car is paid in full, showing signs of wear and tear and you are considering buying a new vehicle in a year or two, consider liability insurance only. This could be risky because you may be caught unprepared to replace your car. Again, this is a personal risk and decision according to what you can afford.

Health Insurance

If you have a large family, insurance is recommended. If everyone is relatively healthy, consider an HMO. The health provider network may be restricted; however, if your doctors and hospitals are in the HMO network, this may be the way to go to save on health insurance costs. Find a reputable insurance agent who can compare the pros and cons of HMO insurance.

Life Insurance

The younger you are, the less expensive your insurance premium.

To determine the amount of life insurance needed for a couple, calculate the amount the surviving spouse would need to pay bills down to an affordable level for the reduced income they will receive. This includes funeral costs as well. As children are born, they should be added too, especially if you don't have $10,000 to $12,000 for funeral costs. Also, decisions must be made between term life and whole life. Term life is generally less expensive but ends at a certain age. If the insured has not died, the insurance ends with no further benefits. But whole life has a date when considered to be paid in full; however, death benefits are still forthcoming. When you build up cash value in the policy, you may withdraw or take loans against the policy. Withdrawals will reduce the policy's value by the withdrawal amount. Also loans require annual interest payments. Some insurance companies (uncertain if this is true for all) will not send payment reminders of the loan payments. The lack of payments and unpaid interest fees also affect the policy's value. It is not recommended to take withdrawals or make loans against the policy. These actions defeat the purpose of acquiring life insurance in the first place.

Homeowner's/Renter's Insurance

Insure your home or apartment against theft, fire, and other disasters. This goes a long way in replacing the contents of your home, and in the case of homeowner's insurance, the home itself. When possible, buy replacement insurance, particularly for the home. The premiums are higher, but in the event of a loss at least you would recover enough funds to replace it.

LEASE VERSUS PURCHASE

Whether looking at a car or a dwelling, you can get into either quicker under the lease option. Car leases normally require a down payment and low, attractive monthly lease rates. The rates are typically lower than you could get into the new car under the purchase option. Pros under a lease car, lower monthly payments, and little maintenance. Cons: If you continue to lease, you will always have a car note. The car must be maintained in pristine condition. Miles must be managed within the annual mileage agreed upon in the lease. When it is time to turn in the car at the end of the lease, you may receive a bill for dents, damage to the interior, and overage of miles. But a car you buy may take 4 to 7 years to pay in full. By the time you pay off a seven-year car note, it is time to look for another due to the high maintenance cost due to wear and tear. However, if you have taken good care of your car, received regular, recommended maintenance, and avoided accidents, you can drive it a couple of years longer than the payment plan.

For homes, again, this is a preference based on what you can afford. If you cannot afford all the maintenance and repairs needed to maintain a home, then apartment living is the best and most affordable option. If you can afford all the homeownership expenses, weigh the pros and cons of apartment living versus single-family dwellings. It is here where preference will weigh more heavily.

OTHER WAYS TO STRETCH THE DOLLAR:

1. Often we see attractive gas prices on GasBuddy, a sales paper placed in our mailbox, or a neighbor shares information about a great sale. The drawback is that the store or gas station is not near your home. Consider the mileage to and from the location and the cost of the gas. If this outweighs the savings, then this may not be a good purchase for you. If, however, the savings are still worth it after you consider the cost of gas, then this may still be a good purchase. Time is also a critical factor in this decision. If you have the time and it is not keeping you from something more important, then time becomes less of a concern. However, if you have a full day, and the other tasks you must do are more important, this may not be a good deal for you.

2. When shopping for clothing or groceries, list what is needed and stick to the list. Lists are outstanding when doing Christmas shopping. List everyone you plan to buy a gift for and determine the amount to spend for each individual. What makes shopping easier is a theme. Let's say this year's Christmas gift-giving theme is comfort. Consider a throw with matching house slippers. If your theme is travel, then travel Accessories such as a nice travel cosmetic bag, with luggage tags and a small handheld scale to weigh luggage. When you have a theme, shopping for everyone is much easier.

3. When possible, do not go to the grocery store hungry. Everything looks delicious. Hunger can lead to all types of unnecessary purchases.

4. When shopping online, beware of purchases made out of the country, particularly in China. It is unfair to say that all Chinese companies are scammers. I have made purchases three times from China. The first experience was perfect. The items were high quality, reasonably priced, and delivered within a reasonable timeframe. However, my second and third experiences were horrible. I ordered an inflatable bed and received a cord. It took several weeks, and when I entered tracking information,

I viewed several negative comments. When I realized that my third purchase was coming from China, I tried cancelling it. I did not receive a refund. When considering a purchase, go directly to the website. Determine if negative comments have been posted. When buying items out of the country, use PayPal or your credit card. Do not use your debit card. PayPal and most credit card companies will work with you to resolve a fraudulent transaction. This is not to say that your bank will not help you with fraudulent transactions, you just don't want to change your bank card or go through any disruptions with your bank account.

> The thoughts of the diligent tend only to plenteousness; But of every one that is hasty only to want.

> Proverbs 21:5

SHOPPING ON CREDIT

> The rich ruleth over the poor, and the borrower is servant to the lender.'

> Proverbs 22:7

There are various reasons as to why individuals shop on credit. Some popular reasons are:

1) You are trying to establish credit.
2) An emergency exists, and no funds are available to address the problem.
3) Something is wanted and we can't wait to purchase the item.

Whatever the reason for using credit, we should go into debt with our eyes wide open. Little debt or the lack of the right mixture of debt could prevent you from getting favorable interest rates. Having too many cards and too much debt can harm you as well. Credit card shopping is more expensive than paying cash. Credit cards have various fees. Delinquent payments incur late charges. Some cards carry annual fees. Most people have debt and need to be aware of how to properly manage it to work in their favor instead of against them. So carefully read this section on spending, and implement as many of the suggestions provided as soon as possible.

HOW TO ESTABLISH CREDIT

The average person entering the workforce for the first time or acquiring their first apartment or car needs financial resources. Many, if not all, turn to credit. Establishing credit should start several months before actually needing it. For example, if you are in college and know you will want an apartment at some point, begin by acquiring credit.

Secured credit card

You could consider a secured credit card. This requires you to put money down as a security deposit to open the account. Your credit limit is tied to the amount of the security deposit.

Unsecured

Research is needed to determine if unsecured credit cards can be obtained.

Credit building tools

Several financial institutions offer credit-building tools but may charge a monthly fee. Experian offers a free credit-building tool, Experian Boost. You may get credit for paying monthly utility, cell phone bills or streaming service bills on time. Contact Experian for ways in which to tie these payments into your credit report.

CREDIT CARDS & INSTALLMENT LOANS

Many use credit cards to purchase necessary and wanted items. It is one thing to use the card to get rewards and pay off the balance within 30 days. (This means that you can afford to make the purchase.) It is another to use the credit card to support spending habits. (This means that the item was not affordable at that time.) It is much more costly to buy items on credit than it is to pay cash. Installment loans work much the same as credit cards, except that once you receive the full amount of the loan, you must begin to repay it. There are no more available funds to draw.

Below is an illustration on how interest adds to the cost of credit card purchases.

ASSUMPTIONS:

1. An item costs $1,000.

2. The annual interest rate is 15.91%. The APR is the annual percentage rate. To determine the rate of interest paid per month, divide 15.91% by 12 (or 1.3258%).

3. Monthly payments are $50.

4. No other charges are made during the period of the outstanding balance.

The $1,000 will cost an extra $169.74 and will take two years to repay.

# of Payments	Payment Amount	Principal	Interest	Balance
1	$50.00	$36.74	$13.26	$963.26
2	$50.00	$37.23	$12.77	$926.03
3	$50.00	$37.72	$12.28	$888.31
4	$50.00	$38.22	$11.78	$850.09

# of Payments	Payment Amount	Principal	Interest	Balance
5	$50.00	$38.73	$11.27	$811.36
6	$50.00	$39.25	$10.75	$772.11
7	$50.00	$39.76	$10.24	$732.35
8	$50.00	$40.29	$9.71	$692.06
9	$50.00	$40.82	$9.18	$651.24
10	$50.00	$41.37	$8.63	$609.87
11	$50.00	$41.91	$8.09	$567.96
12	$50.00	$42.47	$7.53	$525.49
13	$50.00	$43.03	$6.97	$482.46
14	$50.00	$43.60	$6.40	$438.86
15	$50.00	$44.18	$5.82	$394.68

# of Payments	Payment Amount	Principal	Interest	Balance
16	$50.00	$44.77	$5.23	$349.91
17	$50.00	$45.36	$4.64	$304.55
18	$50.00	$45.96	$4.04	$258.59
19	$50.00	$46.57	$3.43	$212.02
20	$50.00	$47.19	$2.81	$164.83
21	$50.00	$47.81	$2.19	$117.02
22	$50.00	$48.45	$1.55	$68.57
23	$50.00	$49.09	$.91	$19.48
24	$19.74	$19.48	$.26	0
TOTALS	$1,169.74	$1,000.00	$169.74	

OBSERVATIONS:

1) Never does the entire $50 payment go towards the original amount borrowed. A part of the payment always goes towards interest.

2) You may pay the credit card off at any time, reducing the amount of interest paid over the life of the debt.

3) In our example, it was assumed that no other purchases were made until the $1,000 was paid in full. In actuality, how many have the discipline to do this?

Also be aware that: 1) late payments are assessed fees. Some companies charge as much as $35. 2) Credit card, mortgage companies and other financial institutions will grant different interest rates to customers based on their credit score. The better the score, the lower the interest rate. The lower the score, the higher the rate. 3) Credit limits and installment loans are based on income, the amount of outstanding debt when the card or loan is issued and the credit score. 4) Credit card companies will always give you a minimum amount due each month. (This maximizes the amount that the credit card companies earn.) The minimum payment is based on a small percentage of the credit card balance or a fixed amount, whichever is greater. A general rule of thumb: If your balance exceeds $1,000, the minimum payment is about 2%. If the balance owed is less than $1,000, then the amount due is about $25. (This can vary from credit card to credit card.) If you owe less than the minimum payment, the entire balance amount will be what is due. WARNING: You never want to pay the minimum. It is costly and could take several years to pay off.

To illustrate this point, let's revisit our example. Still using $1,000, let's use these assumptions:

1) Monthly payments are $25/month, representing the minimum payment. 2) No other charges are made during the repayment period. The repayment period is about 57 months (i.e., more than twice as long as in the previous example.) The cost to borrow over the life of the debt is roughly $440.

3) When applying for credit cards or a mortgage, these companies assess what credit levels you can afford to repay. These might not be aligned with your finances. You need to determine if the payment requirements are something you feel comfortable with. You may have obligations that are not reflected in the data credit bureaus collect. Some examples are helping to care for elderly parents, care for special needs children, special medical conditions, etc. These are important to you and the well-being of your family, but you are the only one with the information to discern the impact on your finances.

4) Mortgage payments include not only the principal amount of the mortgage loan and the interest, but property taxes and homeowner's insurance, as well. It is to the advantage of the mortgage company to know that property taxes are paid and that the property is insured. This protects them from losing their investment. While the mortgage company will determine the principal and interest, the assessor's office will determine your property taxes. It is up to you to shop around for homeowner's insurance. Usually, the mortgage lender will have an estimate for property taxes, and once you select your insurance, one-twelfth will be added monthly to the mortgage payment.

Each year, your mortgage payments may fluctuate. The amounts collected for insurance and property taxes are placed in escrow. These funds are removed from escrow when it is time to pay the insurance and property taxes. (The property tax bills and the homeowner's insurance premiums are mailed to the mortgage company. The borrower also receives a copy for informa-tional purposes.) If, however, there are increases in homeowners insurance or property taxes, the mortgage payments are adjusted accordingly for the following year. If you have a fixed mortgage, your mortgage payments' principal and interest portions never change.

CREDIT SCORES

Once you have established credit, credit bureaus assign a credit or FICO score.

A credit bureau is a company that collects information from lenders on individuals regarding loans, credit cards, repayment history, and credit balances. This information becomes available to other financial institutions, credit card companies, etc. The three major credit bureaus are Experian, Equifax and TransUnion.

FICO, which stands for Fair Isaac Corporation, is a scoring model credit bureaus use to rate an individual's credit. The FICO score, or credit score, is a number that communicates to lenders your credit standing. (Word of caution: not all credit scores are FICO scores. FICO scores are the most popular scores used by lenders.)

A credit score is based on five factors:

Payment History

The payment history tracks the timeliness of payments on credit cards, mortgages, etc. Even one late payment 30 days or more can lower your score. Your bills must be paid on time. An individual's payment history is 35% of the credit score.

Amounts Owed

This factor relates to the total amount borrowed and the amount owed. Paying down a high-balance credit card will positively affect the credit score. The utilization rate for each card is calculated by taking the outstanding balance and divide by the credit limit. An excellent utilization rate is around 10%. This factor represents 30% of your FICO score.

Length of credit history

The longer you have had credit cards and mortgages, the more weight is given to this factor. This indicates the time that an individual has managed his/her debt successfully. This factor represents 15% of your score.

New Credit

This factor measures the number of credit inquiries received by credit bureaus. Be careful of the number of credit inquiries made. Some will affect your credit, and others may not. For example, if you are seeking a loan and apply with various financial institutions within a 30 to 45-day window, these inquiries are considered one, because it is understood that the consumer may shop for a good rate. However, if an individual applies for 6 credit cards within 12 months, this is seen as 6 inquiries and will lower your credit score. Creditors may consider these hard credit inquiries as possible financial distress and elevated credit risk. Inquiries probably have the lowest impact on your credit score. These inquiries could stay on your credit report for up to 2 years but may only impact your credit score for 12 months. This factor is 10% of the FICO score.

Credit Mix

The successful management of multiple debts and different debts helps the credit score. Different debts refer to credit cards, which are considered revolving credit versus installment credit, such as mortgages, student loans, car loans. To have a mixture of credit cards with an installment type of credit is a favorable variable and impacts up to about 10% of your credit score.

A credit score from 300-629 is bad, 630-689 is fair, 690 – 719 is good, and 720 -850 is excellent.

The FICO, or credit score, will help the lender in determining if you qualify for a loan and the interest rate on the loan. The better the score, the lower the interest rates that will be granted.

WAYS TO IMPROVE CREDIT SCORES

You have reviewed your credit report and do not like your credit score. Credit scores are always evolving based on your credit history. Here are some suggestions to improve your credit score:

1. Always make payments on time. If circumstances have caused you to be unable to make your payments on the prescribed due date, talk to the credit card company and negotiate a different payment date.

2. Reduce the number of open credit cards with balances. In an article by cnbc.com published July 17, 2018, entitled 'Here's How Many Credit Cards People With Excellent Credit Scores Have,' persons with excellent credit have about three open credit cards.

3. Keep the debt level to 10% or less of the credit limit. Each credit card has a limit. If the amount owed on the credit card exceeds 10%, getting the balance below 10% will improve your credit score. A second option to improve your score is to talk to the credit card company about increasing your limit until the amount owed is 10% of the new credit card limit. Word of caution: do not use the higher credit limit to increase spending.

4. Review your credit reports. These are obtained from the credit bureaus. Make sure that the information on your reports is correct. If not, contact the credit bureaus and submit whatever is asked to correct the errors on your report. You could have a low score simply because of incorrect information.

5. Catch up on all overdue bills quickly. If you are behind because you can no longer afford the payments, talk to your creditor to find out what payments are acceptable in catching up.

6. Stay on top of your progress. Consider a credit monitoring tool that will send alerts when meaningful changes have been made to your credit score.

7. As your credit rating improves, call your credit card companies and see if you can receive lower interest rates.

WAYS TO REDUCE CREDIT CARD DEBT

1. Determine why your debt is where it is. The cause is clear if it's due to loss of income. Once the income source is replaced, credit card usage should decrease, and debt levels can be reduced. If the problem is the inability to defer self-gratification, then steps must be taken to address this issue. Otherwise, recommendations to reduce debt levels could prove ineffective and cause more frustration. Find someone supportive of your dilemma and willing to offer help to improve the situation. Do not seek help from a shopaholic because this person shares some of your issues.

2. Develop a spending plan. (Refer to spending plan, page 81.)

3. Change your lifestyle. Whatever outings cause your spending, change them. Only go window shopping if you know you will spend money appropriately. Find new pastimes that do not require spending money. If you go shopping every week, reduce it to once a month.

4. Change your credit card strategies. Only use the card for emergencies or items that can be paid in full when the bill arrives. If you can make your purchase with an interest-free offer, ensure you can afford to spread the payments within that period. Provide for your needs and wants from your income.

5. Pay more than the minimum payment. Many credit card companies will provide the number of years needed to pay off your balance if only the minimum is paid. This information is reflected on your monthly credit card statement. The information provided is based on current debt levels. If you continue using the card, this may lengthen the time needed to repay the debt.

6. Increase your current income level and use additional income to align pay more towards your debt.

7. Consolidate your credit cards. Look for credit cards with high credit limits to consolidate your current cards and cards with lower interest rates than your current cards. Consolidating your cards could lower the money being paid out and let you work on more pressing financial goals. Remember to close the cards you have consolidated.

8. Consider bankruptcy if your total debt is twice your annual income. This should be your last resort. Be aware of some downfalls: You cannot borrow for six years, and a Chapter 7 bankruptcy stays on your credit report for about ten years, and Chapter 13 stays on for seven years. Also, if you run up your debts before filing bankruptcy, your petition to file bankruptcy may be denied!

BANKRUPTCY

There are two basic bankruptcy options: Chapter 7 and Chapter 13

Under Chapter 7 bankruptcy, debts, such as credit cards, medical bills and personal loans, are forgiven after three to four months. This option works well for people who have low incomes. (There are formulas used to determine if one's income qualifies). Qualifying assets must be sold. Some assets are protected, such as household belongings. The proceeds from the sale are used to pay creditors.   If there are no assets to sell, the creditors receive nothing.

Under Chapter 13 bankruptcy, a three to five-year repayment plan is developed. Your assets are not sold. This option is typically used by people who earn too much to file Chapter 7, have income to make some payment to creditors and want to address items such as alimony, child support or tax bills that are behind in payments and/or have fallen behind on house or car payments and do not want to lose them. The amount paid to creditors depends on income, expenses, and type of debt.

BEFORE PURSUING BANKRUPTCY, CONTACT A REPUTABLE CREDIT COUNSELOR TO DETERMINE IF YOU CAN PURSUE DEBT RELIEF OPTIONS.

COSIGNING

Be not thou one of them that strike hands,
or of them that are sureties for debts. If thou
has nothing to pay, why should he take away
thy bed from under thee?

Proverbs 22:26-27

Before we discuss the scripture, let's start by describing what cosigning is or being a surety on debt. Cosigning involves someone with good and established credit guaranteeing the debt of another.

Why would someone need a cosigner? The individual applying for the debt does not have good credit, needs more established credit, or there are issues with the level of income.

The word sureties, which appears in the scripture, refers to guarantees that one makes on behalf of another when a loan is involved.

The scripture explicitly states we should never cosign for another. If the creditor is unwilling to grant a loan to the individual on their own merits, you should not as well. The scripture says that if an individual can't afford to pay their debt, the creditor could come after everything the surety has, including his bed.

If the debtor defaults on the loan, the cosigner is on the hook for the debt. To help an individual financially, there are two basic options: give them money or loan them money, but do not cosign on a debt.

Be careful for nothing; but in every thing by
prayer and supplication with thanksgiving
let your requests be made known to God.

Philippians 4:6

SPENDING PART II: PAY WHAT YOU OWE

Render therefore to all their dues: tribute to whom tribute is due; custom to whom custom; fear to whom fear; honour to whom honour.

Romans 13:7

Paying what you owe also includes paying when you owe. Whether an agreement is made with a friend, family member, or company, it is important to pay what is owed when it is due. Communication with the lender is always key when something prevents you from paying what is owed or when it is due. Communicate that you cannot do so at the time but still intend to pay, and provide the date when you can. The lender may offer a suggestion and will greatly appreciate your letting them know about the delay. It is bad faith not to contact the lender at all, even if you still intend to pay. This section will focus on two essential tools to help pay what is owed when it is owed - a spending plan and bank reconciliation.

SPENDING PLANS

A spending plan (or budget) helps you organize and manage your spending. You can see where you plan to spend before receiving the funds. Once you have a plan, you can determine what is needed to reach your financial goals. Some areas can be trimmed, or perhaps you need more funds, or you need to do both.

For some, establishing or living on a plan may be like dieting. It suggests giving up things you enjoy. So you follow it for a while and then fall off the wagon. Just because you follow a plan does not necessarily mean giving up things you like. It means eliminating wasteful spending so more is available for other items. Many I have talked to don't even know how much they spend or what they spend their money on after paying bills. When they spend everything from their paychecks, it is on to their credit cards.

Consider a different, healthier, more worry-free approach to handling your spending. Know what your income is and what your responsibilities are each month. If there are extra funds, work on getting some of those things you want.

When establishing a spending plan, here are the essential parts: Income, tithes (giving), weekly/monthly expenses, and long and short-term financial goals.

At a minimum, create a spending plan for one month. Optimally, it is even better to do it for one quarter. This gives you a broader view of spending needs. For quarterly budgets, as a month ends, delete the completed month from the worksheet and add the new month. Or you might want to print out the completed quarter to compare as you go along. This may be a great boost to continue your plan.

The following example provides a visual example of a spending plan and the rationale for why items are placed where they are.

ASSUMPTIONS:
Mary Doe is a single mother. She works as an office manager and has a son, ten years old.

INCOME
 Funds received weekly, biweekly or monthly determines monthly spending. This includes income earned from a job, child support, pension payments, social security, etc. (A word of caution: If an amount such as child support is not being received regularly, DO NOT include it in the budget until it is received. You can't spend money you don't have!) Also, you may receive

money less frequently, such as income tax refunds. Funds that come in less frequently can buy some things we want or pay down debt to make living more comfortable. Include these items in income in the month in which they are received.

Monthly income is $4,000 per month (before taxes). Mary earns $3,499 from her job and receives $501 in child support. Her payday is on the 15th and last day of every month. The child support payment is received on the 5th of each month. Mary's spending plan has three columns, since she receives funds three times during the month. She would have a column for child support, labelled 5th. Two columns would be provided for her income. One labeled the 15th and one for the last day of the month. (Excel spreadsheets can create your plan, or research apps that can help you with establishing and maintaining your plan.)30% of gross income goes towards payroll taxes, which include FICA, State Income Taxes, and Federal Income Taxes.

Spending Plans are developed according to pay dates and not when bills are due. Schedule your payments on or before when they are due from the nearest income source that precedes the payment.

GIVING

When money is received (except maybe a tax refund), at least 10% should be given. Remember, the Lord asks for tithes and offerings. Your tithes are 10%, and your offering can be whatever you determine.

Mary tithes on her gross income. Before moving forward, let's answer the question as to why you might owe tithes on a tax refund. If you pay tithes on the gross, you already paid the tithe on the refund. This is because your taxes were estimated too high. You paid on the gross, so any refund received has previously been addressed. However, if you tithe on the net or only pay an offering, you owe a tithe on the refund.

EXPENSES

Mary has the following expenses. Each expense is shown with the date it is due.

1. Rent: $1,000 – due 1st of the month. Since the rent is due on the first of the month, it is paid from the check received at the end of the previous month. Water, electricity, gas, and wastewater are all included in the rent.

2. Car Insurance: $100 – due 10th of the month

3. Groceries: The monthly budget for groceries is $300. $100 is purchased on the 5th and an additional $200 of groceries is purchased on the 15th of the month.

4. Cell Phone: $35 per month – due 12th of the month

5. Cable: $45 per month – due 16th of the month

6. Car Note: $325 – due 17th of the month.

7. Two credit cards: The payment of $80 for Credit Card A is due on the 17th of the month and has a $4,000 balance. Credit Card B is also due on the 17th and has payments of $25 per month and a balance of $1,000. We know from our previous discussions on debt that Mary only makes the minimum payments. She is paying $80 on one, only 2% of Credit Card A. Payments on Credit Card B also appear to be the very minimum. Keeping with the 15.91% average interest rate, it will take between 82 and 83 months to repay $4,000, with interest costs over the life of the debt estimated at $2,621.00. (This is a conservative estimate of interest. This will prolong the repayment period. In this example, however, we are maintaining a payment of $80 over the life of the debt and assuming no other charges.) Credit Card B would take about 57 months to repay, with $440 of interest paid over the life of the debt.

8. Internet: $35 per month – due on the 19th

9. Other: Toiletries, cleaning supplies, clothing, shoes, car repairs, unexpected expenses. $150 is set aside for these items on the 5th and 15th. However, at the end of the month, only $39.65 is available for these items.

SHORT/LONG-TERM GOALS

Mary has three financial goals. Her first is to save, the second is to reduce debt, and the third is to provide funds for her child's college education.

Savings

Many of us has experienced an unexpected loss of income, or we know someone who has. Due to the pandemic, many businesses closed their doors permanently. This caused many to lose their jobs. The pandemic was unpredictable, and many who thought their jobs were secure soon learned that the unexpected and the unpredictable can put us in predicaments we never thought would happen. Saving for the unexpected should move to the top of the list.

A general rule of thumb is to save enough to support yourself anywhere from three to six months. Child support will also be considered because as things could happen to Mary and her employment, the same could happen to her child's father. Her monthly income after taxes plus child support is $2,950.30. Three months' salary is $8,850.90. (i.e., $2,950.30 times 3). Mary can only save $239.65 monthly ($60 from child support and $179.65 from the 15th paycheck). It will take Mary about 37 months to save enough to support herself and her son for three months ($8,850.90 divided by $239.65 is 36.9 months).

Reduce Debt

Some may argue that paying off or reducing debt should be Mary's priority instead of savings. Her savings will let her continue supporting herself and her son during a crisis for at least three months, and even though this will only allow her to make minimum payments, she can still manage her debt as she has been.

It will take Mary three years before she can begin to pay off her debt. Now, she has an additional $239.65 that can be used for that purpose. At the end of 37 months, Mary will owe about $438.61 on Credit Card B. She can pay this off in two months. After 39 months of following her spending plan, Mary can now focus on Credit Card A. After 39 months, Mary owes about

$2,646.21. There is $344.65 for Credit Card A payment. ($60 available from child support, $179.65 from the 15th payroll check, $25 used to pay Credit Card B and $80 already in the budget for Credit Card A.) Payments of $344.65 will retire Credit Card A in about eight months.

College Education

46 months later, Mary can now focus on her child's college education. Unfortunately, Mary's child was 10 years old when she started following this plan. Now the child is almost 14 years old, which gives her only 4 years to save for college. As calculated above, she has $344.65 she can save. This will provide $16,543.20 for college. (This does not reflect any interest that may have been earned over the four years.) At today's cost, a four-year in-state public college costs about $22,000. When Mary begins to save four years from now, college costs will be higher. Student loans, scholarships, additional employment are options that Mary must consider with her child. Another option is to work with the child's father to determine if the father can contribute more to the budget to help with college expenses. We are a blended family, and the following arrangement was made for college. The children's natural mom paid for books and weekly spending allowances. Dad paid for tuition and room and board.

Now, let's put this information together.

Due Date	Description	5th	15th	End of Month
	INCOME:			
	Earnings		$1,749.20	$1,749.20
	Payroll Taxes(30%)		($524.85)	($524.85)
	Child Support	$501.00		

Due Date	Description	5th	15th	End of Month
	TOTAL INCOME	**$501.00**	**$1,224.65**	**$1,224.65**
	GIVING:			
	Tithes	$50.01	$174.95	$174.95
	Offering	$5.90	$10.05	$10.05
	TOTAL GIVING	$56.00	$185.00	$185.00
	Expenses:			
1st	Rent (Includes Utilities)			$1,000.00
10th	Car Insurance		$100.00	
	Groceries	$100.00	$200.00	

Due Date	Description	5th	15th	End of Month
12th	Cell Phone	$35.00		
16th	Cable		$45.00	
17th	Car Note		$325.00	
17th	Credit Card A (Balance $4000)		$80.00	
17th	Credit Card B (Balance $1000)		$25.00	
19TH	Internet		$35.00	
	Other	$150.00	$150.00	$39.65
	Total Expenses:	$385.00	$860.00	$1,039.65
	Financial Goals:			
	Savings	$60.00	$179.65	0

Due Date	Description	5th	15th	End of Month
	Debt			
	College			
	Total Financial Goals	$60.00	$179.65	
	TOTAL EXPENSES & GOALS	**$501.00**	**$1,224.65**	**$1,224.65**

FINAL OBSERVATIONS/THOUGHTS ON SPENDING PLANS:

1. Remember that our finances may not always work out as planned. Sometimes, there is no end to things that go wrong. At other times, it seems that we are on a peaceful track. However, you are almost guaranteed never to get to your financial destination without a plan or goal.

2. When saving for future emergencies, life will happen. Occasionally, these funds may be needed before you reach your goal. That's OK. Address the emergency and continue with your plan.

3. If you find it financially uncomfortable after following your initial plan for a month or two, decide what is needed to provide the comfort you seek. There are only two ways to do this: 1) Cut spending or 2) Bring in more income.

4. In the example, every penny has been accounted for. This means that you will always know where you spent your funds. It is optional to show

what you spent in the category labeled other. It is essential, however, to only overspend if you are reducing another flexible area, such as groceries.

5. Paid regularly (faithfully), tithes and offerings will provide surprising results called blessings. These blessings are not always monetary but could result in incredible savings for you and your family. These blessings cannot be planned, nor can you see them coming, but they are welcomed and needed when they do show up. Try it!

BANK RECONCILIATION

Stay on top of your bank balances. You should always know the expenditures made from your bank account before the bank. Track spending and deposits. The more automated your payments, the easier this is to do. Anything that seems fraudulent should be reported to your banker immediately. Take care not to overdraw bank balances. Chronic unpaid overdrafts will make you ineligible for a bank account. Banks and credit unions use ChexSystems, Inc. when potential customers seek to open accounts. If your information in ChexSystems include outstanding fees/charges that you owe other banks you could be prohibited from opening an account. Contact ChexSystems, Inc to find out how you can remove negative information.

Bank accounts should be reconciled at a minimum monthly. Ensure all expenditures per your records agree with what the bank has reported. The same is true for deposits. Always consider any bank fees being assessed. Banks do occasionally make mistakes, so any discrepancies between your records and the banks should be researched. If you still use checks, ensure enough money remains in the account to cover any checks that still need to be cleared.

To illustrate how bank reconciliations are prepared, please review the following example:

ASSUMPTIONS:

Deposits were $1,025

Bank fees are $25 per month

Two checks were written: #101 for $75 and #102 for $50

A $30 automated payment is due in 5 days. No other deposits are expected before it is due.

SAMPLE BANK STATEMENT:		YOUR RECORDS:
Beginning Balance	0	0
Deposit	$1,025	$1,025
Bank Fees	-25	0
Check #101	0	-75
Check #102	0	-50
Automated Payment	0	-30
Balance	$1,000	$ 870

The goal is to review what's recorded by the bank that should be included in your records and vice versa. When the reconciliation has been completed, the bank balance and your records should agree.

SAMPLE RECONCILIATION:

Balance Per Bank Statement	$1,000	Balance Per Your Records:	$870
Outstanding Checks:			
Check #101	-75		
Check #102	-50		
Upcoming Auto Payment	-30		
Bank Fees -			-25
	$845		$845

OBSERVATIONS:

To bring the bank statement into balance to your records, the two checks needed to be deducted, as well as the automated payment. The checks had not yet reached the bank for processing and the $30 automated payment had not been deducted by the bank because it was not due until five days later. However your records reflected the $30 because you don't anticipate receiving anymore funds prior to the due date of the automated payment. Finally your records required adjustment for the monthly bank fees. If the amount is the same each month you don't have to wait until you receive the bank statement to deduct fees from your records. It is best to do it when you receive your last deposit for the month.

Even though many are getting away from checks, it is still important to track your balance independently of the bank balance. Reconciliations are still very much needed. Keep track of the timing and amounts of automated payments and deposits and review bank transactions for fraudulent activity.

The wicked borroweth, and payeth not again.
Psalm 37:21

SAVING AND INVESTING

Go the ant, thou sluggard; Consider her ways, and be wise: Which having no guide, Overseer, or ruler, Provideth her meat in the summer, And gathereth her food in the harvest

Proverbs 6:6-8

These verses encourage us to look closely at the ants and learn from them. After all, Proverbs 30:24-25 refer to ants as being wise. We should look closely at anything the Lord considers wise. Ants are amazing creatures. They are one of the world's strongest creatures in relation to size. A single ant can carry 50 times its body weight. If the ants are interested in a heavier item, they will work together to move it. If men were as strong as an ant, a man weighing 200 pounds could lift 10,000 pounds.

Ants are the longest-living insect. The queen ant, the longest-living ant in the colony, can live several years. The black garden ants can live up to 4 years. Ants are not lazy. Have you ever noticed a group of ants? Some in the colony may carry its load alone, while several may come together to carry a load. Those not carrying anything are scouting. But never will you see an ant standing still.

This next feature causes the scriptures to call the ant wise. Ants prepare and plan. When food is plentiful in the summer, the ant gathers and stores it for winter. The ant has no guarantee it will be alive when winter comes. However, if it is alive, it knows that food is scarce during that time of year, so it relies on the food gathered months earlier.

We will look at the sluggard as we compare him/her to the attributes of the ant. A sluggard is a habitually lazy person. The Bible has a great deal to say about laziness.

Proverbs tells us that:

- A lazy person hates work:

> 'The sluggard's craving will be the death of him, because his hands refuse to work' (21:25)

-He loves sleep:

> 'As a door turns on its hinges, so a sluggard turns on his bed' (26:14)

- He gives excuses:

> 'The sluggard says, 'There is a lion in the road, a fierce lion roaming the streets' (26:13)

- He wastes time and energy:

> 'He who is slothful in his work is a brother to him who is a great waster.' (18:9)

-He believes he is wise, but is a fool:

> 'The sluggard is wiser in his own eyes than seven men who answer discreetly' (26:16)

Proverbs also tells us the end in store for the lazy:

> A lazy person becomes a servant (or debtor): "Diligent hands will rule, but laziness ends in slave labor' (12:24)

- His future is bleak:

> 'A sluggard does not plow in season; so

at harvest time he looks but finds nothing'
(20:4)

- He may come to poverty:

'The soul of the lazy man desires and has nothing; but the soul of the diligent shall be made rich.'(13:4)

A sluggard (or a habitually lazy person) does not prepare themself for the necessities of life. The message here indicates that an ant is not told or guided by a leader, overseer or ruler, yet the ant understands the cycles in his life. The ant realizes that if he is to survive in the winter season, that preparation is required during the summer. While food is plentiful, he gathers provisions for such a time in the year when food is scarce. We, too, have seasons of plenty and seasons of scarcity. Because life normally continues for us longer than the ant, we do not need to wait and see but prepare to the extent we can when opportunity affords. COVID-19 taught us all great lessons about unexpected and extended challenges to health, finances, employment, etc. When the country was informed of the pandemic in late February or March of 2000, none could predict how long the pandemic would last or the far-reaching effects that affected most families worldwide.

So when is the harvest plenteous for humans? When you can still work and are blessed with health and strength. Life has challenges, but none of us know from day to day when we might face them.   We should consider the ways of the ant. Prepare for hard times, such as illness, which prevents us from working, layoffs, a pandemic that closes jobs unexpectedly, etc. Learn to put away something for a rainy day because none of us are promised endless days of sunshine without any of life's storms.

So why save? The reasons for saving are divided into two broad categories. One is a rainy day savings (such as the ant). The other reason for putting money away is for big-ticket items, such as retirement, vacations, weddings, college, furniture, cars, etc. Savings for big-ticket items is considered goal-oriented savings.

RAINY DAY SAVINGS

The rainy day savings should equal three to six months of living expenses. If there is a loss of income, having three to six months of living expenses saved will help significantly in navigating such a loss. These savings should be easily accessible and placed in something liquid. (Liquid in the financial world means it is readily available, preferably without penalty.) For example, you may not want to put your rainy day funds in an annuity with a tax penalty (if you are not of age to withdraw) and taxes on the gains. When you have an emergency, you need as much of the money you have saved as well as immediate access.

GOAL ORIENTED SAVINGS : GENERAL GUIDELINES

Goal-oriented savings should have projected estimates and deadlines. For example, if you are saving to buy a home, how much of a down payment do you want to have on hand? When do you want to buy the home? The amount and the timing will determine when the goal has been met. Or if you are saving for college, how much do you plan to finance, and how much time and money is needed to reach that goal? If you have multiple financial goals, focus on them, estimate them, and determine when you want to reach them.

Also consider which savings or investment instruments work best in meeting your goals. For example, if you are saving for retirement, you might consider a Roth IRA or an annuity. However, if you are saving for college, there are more appropriate tools such as the 529 plan or an ESA. (These instruments will be discussed in greater detail later in this chapter.)

OTHER CONSIDERATIONS IN SELECTING SAVING INSTRUMENTS OR INVESTMENTS:

When selecting one or more options discussed below, answer these questions to determine which one is right for you. If you are interested in multiple options, decide how much you can place in each.

How convenient is it to deposit, access, and manage funds?

If you are considering accounts offered by banks, the more convenient it is for you, the higher the probability of sticking to your savings plan. Not only should you consider the physical location, but how easy is it to manage funds online.

What penalties will be incurred?

Some instruments carry a time commitment. If you are not sure when you will need the funds and are attracted to such instruments, determine if the penalty for early withdrawal is something you don't mind paying. If you do, there may be a better option for you.

If you are investing, do you want a financial advisor or prefer to manage your investments?

When using a financial advisor, you must choose an investment firm and a financial advisor.

What risks are you willing to take with your money?

The higher the return on your money in the stock market, the higher the risk.

How long do you want to invest/save to meet your goal?

If it is less than a year, you may not want to invest; seek the security of a bank product.

THE COOKIE JAR

So, where or how do we start? If you are overwhelmed with bills, pay them down. As your income increases and bills are under control, learn to save as much of your salary increase as possible.

If you could not save anything up to this point due to tight finances, you can still start your savings. We all have loose change. Take a cookie jar, a gallon milk container, an empty bleach container, a piggy bank, and start by taking the loose change you have at the end of the day and place it in that container. Don't go into it until it is full. Empty the container, take it to the bank, and open a savings account. If this isn't working, try cutting out something like cigarettes, morning Dunkin or Starbucks coffee, one junk food snack item, etc. The cost of the item will be saved, and the money you would have used goes into the cookie jar. If you buy coffee every morning, sacrifice one or two mornings. If you buy multiple packs of cigarettes in a week, at least cut back one pack and place those funds in your cookie jar. If you run to the vending machine for a snack every day at work, at least once or twice a week, save those funds and place them in the cookie jar. Find a way to start. This is a slow process, but once you have started, look at more opportunities to grow your money.

No matter what else you do with your funds regarding saving or investing, you may always continue using the cookie jar approach. As you work your way through the maze of decisions and choices for saving and investing, remember you don't have to give up one instrument for another. It is always good to diversify.

As you read these sections, remember to keep your goals in mind and select the best option to meet them.

BANK AND CREDIT UNION INSTRUMENTS

These are standard savings accounts available at most banks and credit unions. Remember that not every bank or credit union has the same offerings.

Regular Savings Account: This is the most common savings account offered. The NCUA (National Credit Union Association) and the FDIC (Federal Deposit Insurance Corporation) insure credit unions and banks, respectively up to $250,000 per depositor and are relatively safe places to deposit funds. Each bank and credit union will determine how many withdrawals per month are allowed and the nominal interest paid on the account.

Online Savings Account: Besides brick-and-mortar banks and credit unions, online banks and credit unions are also available. The online accounts can be managed from smartphones or laptops anywhere. These institutions' offerings must be evaluated like the accounts offered by brick-and-mortar companies.

High-Yield Savings Account: These accounts are like regular savings accounts, except high-interest rates are paid. Shop and compare interest rates and other restrictions or regulations about these accounts.

Certificate of Deposit: Certificate of Deposit (or CDs) normally pay more interest than regular savings accounts. However, they must be held from three months to five years (or longer). The longer the term commitment, the higher the interest rate. Penalties are assessed when an early withdrawal is made. When saving for emergencies, penalties for early withdrawals make CDs less attractive than regular savings accounts.

Money Market Accounts: These funds are also insured for up to $250,000. Money market accounts typically pay less interest than Certificates of Deposit. However, they have more flexibility than the regular savings account. You may access these accounts via debit cards or even checks. They may also require higher minimum balances than other types of savings accounts.

IRA and Roth IRA: IRA accounts are good options for those planning for retirement. Interest rates typically are 7% or 10%, and contributions are limited to $6,000 per year or $7,000 for individuals 50 years and older. The difference between a Roth IRA and a traditional IRA is that a Roth IRA allows you to contribute after-tax dollars, which can be withdrawn tax-free after you turn 59 ½. A traditional IRA allows you to contribute pre-tax dollars, taxed as income, when withdrawals are made the age of 59 ½.

U.S. SAVINGS BONDS

The U.S. Treasury offers two types of bonds: Series EE and Series I.

EE Savings Bonds are reliable, low-risk, government-backed bonds that can supplement retirement income, may be given as gifts, or pay for college education. Bonds sold today earn a fixed rate of interest. Bonds may be held for up to 30 years or until you cash them. They earn interest for 30 years. However, after 20 years, the bonds will be worth twice what you paid. Bonds may be purchased for $25 up to $10,000.

Bonds may be purchased for dollars and cents or even dollar amounts. For example, if you want to buy a bond for $50.23, you can do that. If you prefer to buy the bond for $50, you also have that option. Bonds must be held for one year before cashing them. However, if you cash them before five years, you lose the last three months of interest.

Bonds may be purchased in electronic form from your Treasury Direct Account, or you can buy through payroll direct deposit. Bonds are no longer sold at banks.

The major difference between EE and I bonds is   I bonds carry a fixed and variable rate component to adjust for inflation. They have no guaranteed value at maturity as the EE bonds. You may also buy I bonds by using your Tax Return. All other provisions described above apply to I bonds.

COLLEGE PLANS

These instruments have been developed solely to fund your child's education. One exception is the UTMA (Uniform Transfer to Minors Act) or UGMA (Uniform Gift to Minors Act). These instruments can be used for educational purposes and a wide range of other things that can be used for the child's benefit.

529 PLAN

A 529 plan offers tax-free investment growth and withdrawals for qualified education expenses. Here is some general information about 529 plans.

1. You may open a 529 plan through your state's plan website or through online brokers. However, you are not limited to selecting a plan in the state in which you live. Most states offer 529 plans, and at least 30 states offer tax breaks on contributions. No matter the selected state, your child can go to school anywhere. The exception to this is the prepaid 529 plan. Under this plan, an in-state college is selected, and the tuition

can be prepaid, which will lock in your cost at today's prices. This is only beneficial if you are certain that the school selected is the school your child will attend.

2. The younger your child is when you open a 529 plan, the better.

3. Qualified education expenses include but are not limited to tuition, room and board, textbooks, computers, and printers. The funds can pay for private or religious elementary, middle, and high school tuition. If a withdrawal does not qualify as an educational expense, the withdrawal will be subject to a 10% penalty and ordinary income taxes.

4. 529 plans do not have set contribution limits. However, the IRS guidelines state that the amount necessary to fund the educational expenses cannot exceed what is needed. Even though the IRS does not set specific limits, most states set limits between $235,000 and $529,000.

Coverdell Education Savings Accounts (Coverdell ESA)

A Coverdell ESA is a trust or custodial account set up only for paying qualified education expenses.

1. Like the 529 plan, withdrawals can be made not only to fund a college education but can also finance qualified elementary, middle and high school educational expenses.

2. An ESA can be opened at a brokerage firm or other financial institutions.

3. Contributions are limited to $2,000 per year per child. (This $2,000 limit is based on the filing status and modified adjusted gross income (MAGI). Joint filers with a MAGI of less than $190,000 (or $95,000 for single filers) can contribute up to $2,000. Contribution limits are lower the higher the MAGI is over the $190,000 (Joint) and $95,000 (single) MAGIs.

4. The beneficiary of the account must be under the age of 18 when the account is opened unless the child is considered a special needs child. All funds must be used by the time the child turns 30. If the funds are not

used, all unused funds must be transferred to another child before the original beneficiary (child) turns 30.

5. You can change the beneficiary (child) to another family member. These changes are limited to one per year.

6. If funds are withdrawn for non-qualified expenses, any untaxed earnings are taxable to the beneficiary (child), with a 10% federal penalty.

Uniform Transfer to Minors Act (UTMA) and Uniform Gift to Minors Act (UGMA)

UTMA and UGMA accounts are custodial accounts that can hold funds for minors until they reach majority age. This can range from ages 18 -21 based on state law. The donor must appoint a custodian (or trustee). They may appoint themselves, another person, or a financial institution. The donations are irrevocable and belong to the child.

The most significant difference between the UGMA and UTMA is that the UTMA covers more assets. A UGMA account is limited to purely financial products such as cash, stocks, mutual funds, bonds, other securitized instruments and insurance policies. A UTMA account can hold any form of property, including real property and real estate.

1. The custodian's role is to manage the funds on behalf of the minor.

2. UTMA OR UGMA may be established at a bank or brokerage firm.

3. The income from a custodial account must be reported on the child's tax return and is taxed at the child's rate, subject to the Kiddie Tax rules. The tax return filing is the parent's responsibility; when the child reaches age 14, the child must sign their own tax return.

4. When the child becomes an adult, neither the donor nor the custodian

can restrict how the child uses the funds. The child can use it to start a business, buy a car, pay for their education, etc.

5. There's no limit to the amount you can put into a UGMA/UTMA. But gifts to an individual above $16,000 a year per individual ($32,000 for a married couple) typically require a form to be completed for the IRS.

6. There is no tax benefit to the donor for contributions to a UGMA. These funds are not transferable to another child.

RETIREMENT PLANS

Common investment instruments for retirement planning are 401(K), IRA, and 457. Common features of each are listed below.

401(K)

1. Employers offer 401(k) plans. Employers can make matching or nonmatching contributions to your account. However, some may offer this benefit and make zero contributions.

2. Payroll deductions are tax-deferred.

3. Penalties occur if withdrawals are made before an individual is 59 ½ years old. Mandatory withdrawals must be made by age 72.

4. The federal government determines the amounts an individual can contribute yearly.

IRA

Refer to the section Savings Accounts Offered by Banks and Credit Unions which address IRAs on page 101.

457

A 457 plan is an employer-sponsored plan offered by state and local governments and some qualified non-profit organizations. It offers tax advantages. Contributions to the plan are tax-deferred. An employee may contribute up to 100% of their earnings to the plan, which is done through payroll deductions. Common features include:

1. Employers may also contribute to these plans.

2. Investment options are limited.

3. There may be several fees associated with the plan, which could eat into the interest earned.

4. Funds can be withdrawn at any time without penalty.

INVESTING

Investments may be preferred over bank instruments for long-term financial goals (items that will take more than a year), such as retirement or education.

Before Investing Consider:

Retaining a Professional

Consider a broker or financial advisor. The difference between the two is that a stockbroker buys and sells stock on behalf of clients. Advice is usually offered at the time of trading. Financial advisors provide general and specific financial advice on an ongoing basis. The rest of this section focuses on the financial advisor.

A financial advisor is used to buy and sell stock or invest in mutual funds on your behalf. To find a licensed financial advisor, search for a financial service provider licensed by the DFPI or the Department of Financial Protection and Innovation. The website is https://dfpi.ca.gov or call 1-866-275-2677. This Department protects consumers and services to businesses engaged in financial transactions. The Department regulates a variety of financial services, products, and professionals.

When selecting an advisor, ensure:

a) They are a fiduciary who will act in your best interest. They may push investments on you that earn them the highest commissions if they are not.

b) Find out about their fee structure. Some charge a flat rate, while others may charge a percentage of the account they are managing for you.

c) Find the one with the right expertise for you. If you are interested in saving for retirement, choose an advisor specializing in retirement planning. Most advisors may be able to handle whatever your needs are, but an expert can go the distance on your behalf.

d) Check out their credentials for financial certifications.

e) Make sure your advisor listens to you. They are experts in the financial options available, but make sure they hear your concerns and desires and that you are comfortable with the options selected.

Of all the things to look for in an advisor, I will elaborate on the need for the advisor to consider your views. When my dad retired, he had two options. To receive his retirement in a lump sum payment or receive monthly payments. He selected the lump sum payment and was referred to an advisor by his employer.

For years, his investment grew impressively, and he received monthly payouts. However, his investments were not faring well during the Bush and Obama era. He suffered significant losses. My advice to him was to get out of his current investments and get something that was more stable. His advisor convinced him he would be alright and the market would turn around soon. My father passed, leaving Mom very concerned. My mother trusted my judgment and let me interact with the advisor on her behalf.

We were concerned about her financial survival. Long story short, the investments were changed, the advisor was changed, and while much of their retirement was lost, we salvaged enough for Mom to meet all of her monthly expenses.

Risk- Taking

This is a good segue into risk-taking: Be aware that all investments have risks. Nothing is guaranteed. Whether you hire a financial advisor or do your own trading, you must determine how much of a risk taker you are. Very stable companies have been around for years, and their stocks are considered safe and reliable. There are startup companies that have no historical financial footprints. They may be high-yield but risky. Are you risk-averse? Can you calmly and patiently stand by and watch your investments dwindle? Or can you watch your investments in anticipation of a turnaround, which is not guaranteed but possible? Also, the closer you get to your goal, the less risk you should take. For example, you are saving to buy a home and have given yourself five years to save. You have selected a high-growth, high-risk stock which has performed well in the first three years. You have two years left before you are ready to make that big purchase. Consider a slower growth investment. Or track the performance of the investment often. When you see it begin to decline, sell.

None of us can predict what will happen to our investments. Several factors could cause investments to lose money. The company and or top officials could be named in a scandal. The Announcement of a large product lawsuit or recall, etc. Some events have short-term effects, others much longer. You do not want the gains you've made to be wiped out. Even though you have a financial advisor, you should receive statements regularly on how your investments are doing. Talk to your advisor and learn how to read and interpret the information being shared with you.

Self-Investment

Select A Company: There are several internet investment companies. Use the internet to help select the company of interest to you. Review any comments that may be available. Find out if fees are charged. If so, how much and when?

Select your stock portfolio: There are several ways to select stock you want to invest in. You may choose your favorite store, or a company involved in products or services of interest, new up-and-coming companies, companies made on referral, etc. Once you pick a stock, do a little research to determine how it is performing.

Basic Trading Information: Find a tutorial explaining basic terms you need to familiarize yourself. Whatever the reporting information or indicators being received from the trading company, study the meaning so you may effectively manage your account.

Buy or Sell: Determine when you want to buy or sell a stock. Some internet investment companies will let you set limits. For example, if you buy a stock for $30, you may set a limit of $25. If the stock reaches $25, alerts are sent so you can sell.

CRYPTOCURRENCY

Cryptocurrency is a growing market and has captured the attention of many young investors. It is a virtual currency. You can hold it for investment purposes or use it as a form of cash for certain purchases.

One risk of cryptocurrency is cryptocurrency exchanges. Exchanges such as Coinbase make buying and selling crypto assets easy. The drawback is that many people don't like to keep their digital assets on exchanges due to the control the company has over allowing access to your assets. An exchange could freeze your assets due to a government request or go bankrupt, leaving you with no recourse in retrieving your money.

This currency can be stored offline using cold storage options like hardware wallets. The most significant risk with this option is losing your private key. Without the key, your assets cannot be accessed.

However, despite the risks, cryptocurrencies are growing stronger. Much-needed financial infrastructure is being built, and professional and individual investors are gradually receiving the tools to manage and safeguard their crypto assets.

If you should invest in cryptocurrency, you must assess the investment as you would any other. If you believe cryptocurrency usage will become increasingly widespread over time, including it as part of your investment portfolio may make sense. Do not invest all of your funds in cryptocurrency at this time. More regulations are needed, and cryptocurrency requires more of a track record. If you do your research and contend that it is too risky, but you want to get your feet wet, consider buying stocks of companies with exposure to cryptocurrency, such as Coinbase, PayPal, etc.

DIVERSIFY INCOME

Income from employment and savings does provide some income diversification. However, the advice provided in Ecclesiastes 11:2 will serve to strengthen financial viability particularly during adversity.

Give a portion to seven, and also to eight; for thou knowest not what evil shall be upon the earth.
Ecclesiastes 11:2

Different bible translations use different words for portion. We will look at a couple which, hopefully help us to understand what is being said. Instead of the word portion as used in the King James translation, ventures is used in the NIV or New International Version. NET or the New English Translation says: Divide your merchandise among seven or even eight investments. These translations appear to point to the need to diversify income 7 or 8 different ways.

Chapter 11 of Ecclesiastes highlights the fact that God is in control. He is the only one that knows what will happen. He is urging us to make the most of our opportunities. Are you familiar with the saying: Don' t put all of your eggs in one basket. This is a call to do just that. The goal is the establishment of seven to eight income streams.

To acquire seven or eight income streams is not as difficult as it may sound. For example, if you are employed and save, you have established two income streams. If you have a spouse who is also employed, you have three sources of income. Add 401(k)s to one or both spouses. You have now established one or two more sources of income. Look at investing in different stocks or mutual funds. These suggestions taken together can provide seven or eight sources of income.

Saving and investing aren't the only means to diversity income. Look at your resources and skill sets and see how they may be used to supplement your income.

It is rare, that we can enter adulthood, begin our work career and develop seven or eight income sources from day one of employment. This financial principle will take some time to accomplish; however you may be able to start with at least two (i.e . employment income and the establishment of a savings account.

There be four things which are little upon the earth, But they are exceeding wise: The ants are a people not strong, Yet they prepare their meat in the summer

Proverbs 30:24-25

WHY DO I SPEND?

I spend because I have some time.
I spend 'cause I can't keep a dime.
I spend so I can have one too.
I spend because there's nothing else to do.

I spend because this is out of style.
I spend because I've had this for awhile.
My friend just bought a new car.
Mine will be bigger and better by far.

All of my clothes are just not right.
I need a new dress to go out tonight.
I need new jewelry with larger stones.
Now I'm in need of payday loans.

My phone is six months old.
But the new upgrades are amazing. I'm sold.
Nike has a new shoe in the store.
I'm going to buy 2 pairs or more.

I went to the store and bought four
It was on sale, I didn't need more
The thirty that I have stashed away
Are being saved for what? I can't say.

I spend when I am ten feet off the ground
I spend when I'm lonely and no one's around.
I spend to celebrate good fortunes with you
Oh who am I kidding any reason will do.

Now I look in the mirror and oh what a shame
I messed up my credit and tarnished my name
Bankers, and creditors and lenders alike
Cause me to hide and duck out of sight

Now I'm not sick at least that's what I say
So I pray oh God send help my way
My prayers He'll answer and that I can trust
If only I could stop this material lust.

The dollar bill has more faith than I do
In God We Trust, is clearly in view
In Proverbs, the ant is smarter than me
He stores up food for a winter he can't see.

I know my bills should be paid on time
My spending should be planned to the very last dime
Then I could answer my phone when it rings
And discover the peace that responsibility brings.

Jesus Christ, My Lord and Savior
Has never left me because of bad behavior
After all I've done, he loves me still
Even though I need help with the dollar bill.

I need to change. I need a fresh start
With a tenth, I'll give with a cheerful heart.
After that I'll pay all my bills on time
And start to save a nickel or even a dime

The next time we talk about my spending
My story will have a better ending
I'm ready. I am armed with His plan.
My finances I now place in His hands.

CONCLUSION

Better is the end of a thing than the beginning
thereof
Ecclesiastes 7:8

Take a moment to reflect on God's plan:

Stewardship: How well we use our time, talents and financial resources shows our commitment or lack thereof to the Lord. Acknowledge and accept your role as God's steward. All we have comes from Him so treat all blessings responsibly and wisely. When we sincerely accept our role as His steward, we can adjust our actions accordingly.

Financial Pitfalls: Your attitude towards money will drive your behavior. Remember to avoid laziness and the love of money.

Giving: Give faithfully, regularly, cheerfully and generously. Give your best and not what is leftover.

Spending: Spend wisely. Buy what you can afford. Buy at the best price. Always prioritize and address your needs over your wants. Pay what you owe and pay on time.

Saving/Investing: Don't spend all of your money. Become ant wise! Diversify income sources.

So how do we get started. If you are new on this financial journey start following the principles presented starting from the front of the book and work your way to the end. If you have been managing your finances for some time and need to address some areas, pick one, and implement the necessary changes. With prayer and perseverance you can do it!

Finally, following God's plan is no guarantee that the storms of life wil not come. However, following God's plan wil be of great assistance to you and your family. Whatever life challenges you face, remember God's promise to you:

31 Therefore take no thought, saying, What shall we eat? Or, What shall we drink? Or, Wherewithal shall we be clothed?
32... For your heavenly Father knoweth that ye have need of these things.
33 But seek ye first the kingdom of God, and his righteousness ; and all these things shall be added unto you.
34 Take therefore no thought for the morrow: for the morrow shall take thought for the things of itself...
Matthew 6:31-34

ABOUT THE AUTHOR:

Carolyn Keith is a dedicated Christian, who wears many hats. In addition to being the pastor's wife, she serves as the church's financial secretary, the teen Sunday school teacher, and the retreat and summer camp chair. Carolyn is a Certified Public Accountant and holds a Bachelor's Degree in Accounting and a Master's Degree in Management, Finance and Marketing. She has over 20 years of experience at the executive level in the finance and accounting fields. The culmination of the two vocations (i.e. Christian and Certified Public Accountant) led to God's Bailout Plan.   She lives with her husband, Lloyd, in Northwest Indiana.

MESSAGE FROM THE AUTHOR:

I feel very privileged to have shared this time with you. Everyone that reads this book is in a different place with their finances. Some have managed very well, and was just curious to see how their money management skills aligned with God's Bailout Plan. Some needed just a little help and some of you needed much more. Wherever you are with your finances, it is my prayer that something presented within these pages has been helpful. It is my desire that you will as soon as you can align your financial practices with God's plans for you.

CONTACT THE AUTHOR:

Visit website: www.vineyardministry.org
Email: cvkeith@vineyardministry.org
Phone: 1-219-256-9400

www.ingramcontent.com/pod-product-compliance
Lightning Source LLC
Chambersburg PA
CBHW060618200326
41521CB00007B/800